God, Death, Art and Love

The Philosophical Vision of Ingmar Bergman

ROBERT E. LAUDER

Prologue by Liv Ullmann

Paulist Press
New York and New Jersey

Photos are used by permission of the Museum of Modern Art,
Film Stills Archives, New York City.

Book design by Nighthawk Design.

Copyright © 1989 by Robert E. Lauder

Library of Congress Cataloging-in-Publication Data

Lauder, Robert E.
God, death, art, and love : the philosophical vision of Ingmar
Bergman / by Robert E. Lauder.
p.   cm.
Includes bibliographical references.
"Selected filmography": p.
ISBN 0-8091-3108-0 :   (est.)
1. Bergman, Ingmar, 1918–   —Criticism and interpretation.
2. Bergman, Ingmar, 1918–   —Philosophy. I. Title.
PN1998.3.B47L38   1990
791.43′0233′092—dc20
[B]   89-37263
                                                          CIP

Published by Paulist Press
997 Macarthur Boulevard
Mahwah, New Jersey 07430

Printed and bound in the
United States of America

DEDICATION

To Tom and Pat
with gratitude for years of friendship,
and
to Katie and Nora with hope.

Like countless others I am grateful to Liv Ullmann for her extraordinary talent and for her many exceptional screen and theatre performances. I am also grateful to her for her marvelous work for children all over the world as Ambassador of Good Will for UNICEF. Of course I am grateful to her for writing the Prologue to this book but I am especially grateful to her for the special gift of her friendship.

R.E.L.
July 1989

Acknowledgements

Excerpts from *Four Screenplays of Ingmar Bergman* by Ingmar Bergman, copyright © 1960, 1988 by Ingmar Bergman are reprinted by permission of Simon and Schuster, Inc. Excerpts from *Bergman on Bergman* by Stig Bjorkman, Torsten Manns and Jonas Sima, translated by Paul Britten Austin, copyright © 1979 by P.A. Norstedt and Soners Forlag, translation copyright © 1973 by Martin Secker and Warburg Ltd. are reprinted by permission of Simon and Schuster, Inc. Excerpts from *Fanny and Alexander* by Ingmar Bergman, translated by Alan Blair, English translation copyright © 1982 by Alan Blair are reprinted by permission of Pantheon Books, a division of Random House, Inc. Excerpts from *Autumn Sonata* by Ingmar Bergman, translated by Alan Blair, translation copyright © 1978 by Alan Blair, are reprinted by permission of Pantheon Books, a division of Random House, Inc. Excerpts from *A Film Trilogy* by Ingmar Bergman copyright © 1988 by Ingmar Bergman are reprinted by permission of Marion Boyars Publishers, New York and London. Excerpts from *Persona and Shame: The Screenplays of Ingmar Bergman* by Ingmar Bergman translated by Alan Blair, translation copyright © 1984 by Alan Blair are reprinted by permission of Marion Boyars Publishers, New York and London.

Contents

Prologue: *The Man Who Lives on an Island*

LIV ULLMANN

INGMAR BERGMAN—the storyteller of soul—forever seeking "the high mountain, the vast cloud, the silent forest, and the rippled spring."

His grandmother's travels with him into the wonders of Fairy Tales.

Which he continued alone when she died. Alone—and then sometimes with company.

And on one of these travels we met. He with a heavier set of luggage than I (some of which he left me with when we parted), both of us seeking paths of the "wonderful" that old women, our grandmothers, had pointed out to us.

On the first excursion together on an Island new to both, we were in love, thus only a couple of films were made. At that time, nothing existed outside of ourselves.

There was no joy or pain which had not been inflicted by the other.

He took my hand in his and said: "I had a dream last night. That you and I are painfully connected." On the spot where we were sitting he built his house, and all that had formerly been my life was unreal and far away. I wondered what would become of me.

1

Ingmar once wrote in a book something about my ability to put feeling into any part of my body, calling it "an extraordinary technical accomplishment," then illustrating his point by noting that in *Persona* he asked me to put the feelings of one specific scene into my lips—and then watched my lips get bigger.

Thus, many years later I went to see *Persona*—waiting to see an enormous revelation on my lips. I couldn't see it.

He was searching for something on an island where people lived close to the earth, close to the sea, close to that which may seem natural and predetermined for us. But with the exception of a few documentaries from the Island, his films would continue to reflect the young child's soul and the journeys to the forest and the springs and the clouds of the dreams where he had wandered in his childhood. Reflect the sacrifices and all the pain of those days. Tears accumulated as if they had been suffered for "thousands and thousands of years."

He managed to live in harmony with his own self. Even though his films and his need for solitude did not seem to reflect such harmony. He managed to live with everything that was good *and* evil in him.

No outsiders could point to him and make him feel inferior—not really—not even a travel companion.

He was not without demands or hatreds or aggressions. But such pride—such pride he allowed no one to crush.

His roots had been lodged in a childhood so long ago, moistened or withered by the experiences of those days.

An Islander in our society. The way children are, a feeling of simple security—which may be the dignity of the heart.

Children are without self-consciousness. It is like when a child first makes a painting, with innocence, with a pure soul. The child says: a tree is that black dot with all the red things around it, and not before ten people have told the child that trees don't look like that does he look at his dots and never paints again. . . . The great potters say that adults would not have the freedom or innocence to just do a tree as two lines.

In Ingmar's life this peculiar innocence and naiveté of his has sometimes worked against him.

It also happens to be his strength. Because he is in touch with something inside of himself that many are not close to, although they might be wiser or better read or better adjusted to life than he is, though no one can be more creative.

A man of solitude. An islander.

For him, loneliness has worked because it kept him choosing what his grandmother let him glimpse at.

The land of shadows and sun stripes and velvet and tears.

The sheep on his island stay out of doors all year; like the landscape on which they live, they look like survivors from another time. Curiously shaped heads, big bodies heavy with wool that drags along the ground.

When they give birth in March, the temperature may be 30 degrees below zero.

Ingmar would spend hours watching them—talking about them—wondering what they felt—as if he was finding parallels to his childhood—his own memories of survival.

One day we stood completely helpless looking at the drama of life and death in nature. The wind lashed our faces. It was dark and stormy, a lamb was hanging from the mother's body while she stood waiting, her head bowed to the wind. It was no sooner born and the mother's tongue had touched it, than a second lamb arrived. And now it was the survival of the fittest. The mother began licking the last arrival which was considerably larger. The smaller one remained lying on the ground, while blood and slime turned to ice on the little body.

"Oh," Ingmar whispered and his face was so young—with such pain written on it. "Oh," he whispered.

He stepped forward—making an awkward attempt to help, but only succeeded in frightening the mother away. He withdrew. Watched. Watched the first born lying still on the ground. Cautiously, the mother came back—licked her biggest child—until, dry and on thin and wobbly legs, it rose to test the world.

That evening the farmer collected three dead lambs the flock had left behind as they continued their slow trek through the evergreen forest.

Pictures—which are fragments of our life together: walks on the beach, when like children we buried coins in the sand so that we could find them again many years later. In case we were poor or war had come. A small pile of stones in memory of a summer day and of two people who knew how to play together.

I sought the absolute security, protection. Of course, that was not *there*—on his Island.

He sought someone like the grandmother. Arms that would open to him, warm and without complications. His dream was the woman—like her—who had been created in one piece. But *I* crumbled into all kinds of bits and pieces if he wasn't careful.

His hunger for togetherness was insatiable.

I have a childhood picture of Ingmar. He is standing in the middle of a row of thirteen-year-old boys. I can see that his skin is pimply, recognize the loneliness and the bashfulness, and believe I can sense his feeling of being an outsider.

Once we were invited to dinner by a rich producer in Rome. We were supposed to be the only guests, but within half an hour the host's large apartment was filled with people who had been invited to meet Ingmar at close range. Then he had the same expression as in the picture. He was pale when he told the producer he had to leave at once. The others sat down for dinner without the guest of honor.

He is the young boy chasing the unknown on an endless road, in a world he describes in his grandmother's Fairy Tale as "a stony plain where nothing grows. The fiery sun burns from morning to evening and nowhere can the people find any coolness or shade."

And because I was once one of his travel companions, I know with what urgency he would ask *where* we were going. Where his "native land and the final goal for his wanderings" might be.

We recognized so much in each other. Perhaps we were too much alike.

Sometimes he said that we were.

He told me once I reminded him of his grandmother. His grandmother. Mine sang for me—so did his.

In the nape of his neck I find the sweet and dusty smell of mine, yes—just the same. We used to think that was a sign. That our grandmothers sat in heaven and pointed us out to each other.

My grandmother is sitting in an armchair. On her lap is a little girl, me. Or is it Ingmar?

Soft children's hands caress old and bony ones.

Stories of spring and of grass that is apple green, and marguerites that can answer your questions and blackbirds which hide in holes and crows that try to sing.

In our childhood we both met animals that talked, and so did trees and stones.

Always encountered with our grandmothers—then.

He tells me of a lap; it is very warm and safe. There he sits. Look at that faint, proud smile. Embraced by aged arms.

I see in him the beauty of another childhood so many years ago.

Of tears that were really treasured pearls concealed in eyes. So he was told—and I was too.

And like a miracle, when tears appear it's good and safe. Setting free everything that hurts far inside a little boy or little girl—inside the red, velvet room where all sorrow and all happiness exist together.

As a grownup he could never cry. I saw him crying only twice.

Once, when his mother died. For a short time there in my arms his hurt flowed free.

I lived on his Island for a period of my life—in a strange world of fragrances and colors that only gradually revealed themselves. But our real journey together in search of the wonderland happened only after I left the Island and him.

Only then could I understand his need to find the "deep clear springs where you can slake your thirst, where you can bathe your burning face, where you can cool your blistered feet."

Yes, then I truly saw and understood how much alike we were and why we could work together.

And be friends.

I have wondered who I would have been if I had not had him as a travel companion for such a long time in my life—once as my lover, and then for a much longer time—telling stories together.

The experience of having seen into the soul of a young boy and being full of tenderness for what I found.

For a period of time we held each other's hands and were painfully connected.

But only when it was all over did we become true friends.

"What unknown destination?" I asked when we met.

"I was there once when I was young," he answered, "now I am trying to find my way back."

I wonder what his grandmother thinks if she can watch his continuous journey seeking "the high mountain, the vast cloud, the silent forest, and the rippled springs."

Oh—how I wonder what our grandmothers think. . . .

Introduction: *Encountering Cinema's Genius*

ANOTHER BOOK ABOUT Ingmar Bergman. Why? With a touch of philosophical whimsy I am tempted to answer my rhetorical question with another question: Why not?

It is probably impossible to overestimate the role that art plays in social intercourse. In a real and indispensable way the great artist, by mirroring our preoccupations and expressing our deepest needs and desires, tells us who we are. In an historical period's art the researcher can find the people's images of themselves. The great works of art are the words, articulated by geniuses, that people wish to say about themselves. James Joyce's succinct expression of his own vocation can serve as a good self-description of every great artist: "Welcome, O life! I go to encounter for the millionth time the reality of experience and to forge in the smithy of my soul the uncreated conscience of my race."[1] Not only do the great artists deeply influence the consciousness and conscience of people, but they also speak for the rest of us. Psychologist Rollo May has written:

But those who present directly and immediately the new forms and symbols are the artists—the dramatists, the musicians, the painters, the dancers, the poets, and those poets of the religious sphere we call saints. They portray the new symbols in the form of images—poetic, aural, plastic, or dramatic, as the case may be. They live out their imaginations. The symbols only dreamt about by most human beings are expressed in graphic form by the artists. . . .

9

Thus the artists . . . are a "dew" line, to use McLuhan's phrase; they give us a "distant early warning" of what is happening to our culture. In the art of our day we see symbols galore of alienation and anxiety. But at the same time there is form amid discord, beauty amid ugliness, some human love in the midst of hatred—a love that temporarily triumphs over death but always loses out in the long run. The artists thus express the spiritual meaning of their culture. Our problem is: Can we read their meaning right?[2]

This book is an attempt at reading one artist aright. No film director in the last thirty years has had as much print devoted to discussions of his work as Bergman. Birgitta Steene's excellent bibliographical treatment of Bergman materials[3] reveals the fascination that he has held for cineastes since he achieved an international reputation in 1956, the year his *Smiles of a Summer Night* won a prize at the Cannes Film Festival. Not only have countless articles appeared about Bergman but he has been the subject of more than forty books. Is not one more book doomed to be superfluous? Can anything more be said about the Swedish genius?

Without being the least defensive or self-effacing I can admit not only that my book will not be the last about Bergman but that even its author is delighted it will not be. I believe that to close off future treatments of Bergman's films would be analogous to closing off treatments of Shakespeare and Joyce. It is quite possible that cinema will some day have another creative artist of Bergman's stature.[4] I hope it does. But until it does, Bergman is in a class by himself. He is to film what Shakespeare is to theater, and Joyce is to literature. I agree with critic John Simon's assessment of Bergman: "Ingmar Bergman is, in my most carefully considered opinion, the greatest film-maker the world has seen so far."[5] Cinema has had other directors who were geniuses, but the number of cinematic masterpieces that Bergman has created give him a privileged position in the history of cinema. That Bergman is also the author of every film, save one, that he directed over the last thirty years highlights his accomplishment.

Not only is Bergman a cinematic genius but he is a *contemporary* cinematic genius. Even an author who has serious reservations about Bergman said the following about his artistic accomplishment:

You may be able to name other film artists who surpass Bergman in subtlety, in urbanity, in exuberance, in courtesy of heart, and in scope of social interest; you can choose directors whose styles you favor for their camera inflections, their tempo, their modes of composition, and their rhythms; you will find few who have anything like Bergman's obdurate and sustained integrity; none who has so artfully succeeded in displaying his temperature chart as a map of the world. In his own boreal and phobic way, Bergman has engaged that subterranean crisis of the spirit which we have agreed to call modern. . . .[6]

That books will continue to appear about Bergman is to be expected. But why this book? That Bergman has made his last film and that his autobiography recently appeared[7] would seem to make this discussion of the author/director especially timely. Not only are we guaranteed that no new work will be added to the corpus of Bergman's cinematic creations but we now have his own report and reflections on his life. However, I am hoping that my extended essay has more justification than mere timeliness. This is one of the few books devoted entirely to a discussion of Bergman's philosophic vision,[8] written by a professional philosopher from a philosophic standpoint. From the time I first viewed *The Seventh Seal* approximately thirty years ago and became fascinated by what I thought Bergman was saying through his art, I have thought that his work, more than that of most directors, demands the most radical questions. Bergman's films deal with philosophic questions, and therefore light should be shed on the films by reflecting on them philosophically. That is the premise that motivated me to write this treatment of Bergman.

One last but not the least prefatory note about our examination and evaluation of Bergman's philosophic vision: Even though Bergman's films deal with philosophy we can still ask whether those films deserve the attention of the philosopher. Approximately a decade away from the millennium is there a value in philosophizing about film? The world is wracked with serious problems. Almost one-third of the human race is suffering from malnutrition. We are living under the shadow of a possible nuclear holocaust. The drug problem seems worse than ever. The poor and the homeless surround us with pleading eyes. There is violence in the streets, corruption in government, educational crises in our institutes of higher learning. A case could be made that Western civilization is on the brink of collapse. In the face of these pressing problems how can philosophizing about films be justified? Can musing about movies be more than a scandalous waste of time?

Without in any way either minimizing any of the important problems that plague us, or excusing ourselves, or forgetting that we are our brothers' keepers and without being facetious, I wish to suggest that some wasting of time is important precisely at this moment in history. The nature of philosophy is tied to a kind of "wasting time." To philosophize requires some leisure, and indeed philosophizing can reveal not only the meaning of leisure but the meaning of ourselves. In his classic *Leisure the Basis of Culture*, Josef Pieper puts both leisure and philosophy into proper perspective. What Pieper stresses is that leisure should not be thought of as doing nothing but rather as allowing yourself to do what is most human. It is not to be confused with laziness or what the medievals called *acedia*, which really prevents persons from being at peace with themselves.[9] Leisure is the opposite of a restlessness that leads to work for the sake of work. Pieper wrote:

Leisure, it must be clearly understood, is a mental and spiritual attitude—it is not simply the result of external factors, it is not the inevitable result of spare time, a holiday, a week-end or a vacation. It is, in the first place, an attitude of mind, a condition of the soul, and as such utterly contrary to the ideal of 'worker' . . .[10]

Pieper says that leisure enables someone to come "to full possession of his faculties, face to face with being as a whole."[11] Paradoxical as it seems amidst all the problems that abound in the contemporary world and that cry for our intervention, what Pieper calls leisure is crucial. If we want a better world we need to reflect on what we mean by "better." An activism that disregarded serious thought about ultimate matters such as God, death, freedom, love, would probably increase and intensify our problems. That philosophy always buries its undertakers is true.[12] What Bergman provides for us is several artistic masterpieces that can invite serious reflection from a viewer.

I am aware that it is paradoxical that this value be attributed to his work because in the past Bergman has been accused of narcissism and of creating out of too private a world. At this moment a rampant individualism is one of the more serious problems in the United States. In *Habits of the Heart* Robert Bellah and company have identified frightening currents of individualism in both private and public life.[13] Christopher Lash in his *The Culture of Narcissism* identified the presence of narcissism throughout our culture.[14] There is evidence that much of contemporary American cinema is infected with narcissism. The paradox of Bergman's work is that the Swedish genius deals with the dramatic situations which, when reflected upon, call us out of ourselves into a wider community. Bergman's questions about and dramatization of love at the very least pose serious alternatives to an audience. I have views on God, death, art and love that are quite different from Bergman's, but I think that viewing and reflecting on Bergman's films have greatly affected my philosophy of God, death, art and love. It is true that Bergman dramatizes his personal preoccupations. Vernon Young's approach to Bergman's films is basically acceptable. The critic wrote:

For myself, I have learned in Bergman movies always to look for the personal involvement first. His subject, whatever ramifications and ideal extensions may be suggested, is forever himself.[15]

My experience has been that philosophizing about Bergman's films can raise all the important questions. Raising the important questions is part of being human; having the courage to live by your answers to those questions is what makes the human journey an adventure. Bergman as artist is not a narcissist nor do his films foster narcissism. The opposite is the situation: Bergman explores what is universal and his films can call us to deeper appreciation of our common humanity.

My study of Bergman does not deal with his work in the theater[16] nor does it deal with all of Bergman's films. I start with *The Seventh Seal* (1957) because I believe that the films that preceded it, while interesting to study,[17] in general cannot compare with the work that followed. I exclude *All These Women* (1964) because it is a comedy, *The Magic Flute* (1975) because it is more Mozart than Bergman, the two Faro Documentaries (1970 and 1979) and the short film *Daniel* (1967). I include only films that appeared in theaters even if they may have first appeared on television. When a Bergman film appeared in both media I refer only to the theater version. Though I liked *After the Rehearsal* (1984) better than *Fanny and Alexander* (1982), I exclude the former work and consider Bergman's corpus of films to have ended with *Fanny and Alexander*. In this I am following Bergman's wishes that *Fanny and Alexander* be considered his last film.[18] So I am discussing the films from Bergman's classic period[19] from *The Seventh Seal* to *Fanny and Alexander*, a period of twenty-five years of extraordinary creativity. While I will make some reference to every film in that period I will not discuss every one in detail but rather explore films in terms of the four topics that I think capture Bergman's preoccupations: God, death, art and love. Though I believe that I could use almost any of the films from *The Seventh Seal* to *Fanny and Alexander* to illustrate my points concerning Bergman's philosophical vision, I admit that the actual films chosen in any chapter are due to a combination of my taste, my aesthetic judgment concerning a particular film and my decision concerning which films best illustrate Bergman's vision on one of the four topics. Therefore I plead guilty to the charge that my choices are at least a bit arbitrary. To deal in detail with each of the four topics in relation to each Bergman film would lengthen this study and I fear lessen its readability. I believe I have discussed Bergman's films in sufficient detail to make clear just what Bergman's philosophical vision as dramatized in his films is. When I quote from the films I rarely rely on my memory but more often use the published text of the film.

I have written this book for anyone who is interested in Western culture. Bergman is such an extraordinary talent and has so successfully dramatized the philosophical preoccupations and personal problems of so many of his contemporaries that I think his stature as a spokesman-artist for the third quarter of the twentieth century is unrivalled. Anyone interested in examining the intellectual history of the last thirty years must not overlook Bergman. This book is also written for actual or potential lovers of film. For those who have seen Bergman's films my hope is that my treatment will motivate them, whether they agree or disagree with me, to reflect on Bergman's artistic output and indeed to examine their own philosophical vision. For those who have not seen Bergman's films my hope is that the book will encourage them to go to the source that has provoked my writing and allow that source to provoke them to deepen and broaden their philosophical vision. With the naivete of a parent hoping in an offspring, I visualize the book being used in film courses, philosophy courses and even religious studies courses. I am not so naive as to think I have done justice to Bergman but in fantasy I characterize myself as a contemporary Socrates outside a movie house which is running a Bergman festival. I am encouraging people to attend and also posing a few questions to those leaving the theatre.

1

Metaphysical Meanings and the Movies

ROBERT JOHANN'S description of philosophy is one of my favorites:

Of all human enterprises, philosophical inquiry is the most practical. It is the use of intelligence to liberalize action, to open up new possibilities.

Philosophy is also passionate. It is spurred by dissatisfaction with what needs correction, zeal in the communal search for greater sense, joy at new harmonies achieved. It is mind in the service of heart, a discipline in the service of human growth.

Philosophical inquiry is, at its best, an adventure in making life whole.[1]

Accepting Johann's description we can say that every person engages in philosophical inquiry. The professional philosopher might do it through research or teaching or writing but every person tries to make sense of his or her life, to engage in activities that lead to growth, to make life whole. Bergman as part of the human race is no exception.

As a preface to presenting my own philosophical vision, which presentation itself will serve as a preface to our discussion of Bergman's philosophical vision, I wish to reflect briefly with the reader on the concepts of mystery, intentionality, horizon and

dialogue. Reflection on these four topics will involve us in philosophical thinking and introduce the reader to my philosophical
vision of God, love, death and art.

Philosophy is personal in a way that other intellectual disci-
plines are not. Existentialist philosopher Gabriel Marcel has
provided illuminating insights that may help us to see why philosophy is a unique outlook on reality. Marcel made a distinction
between a problem and a mystery[2] and pointed out that whereas
science deals with problems, philosophy deals with mysteries.
According to Marcel there were four differences between problem and mystery.

A problem is exterior to the self. It is out there. In that sense it
is objective. A scientific problem is exterior to the scientist and
though it may demand a great deal of his attention, he is not
included in the problem, he is not part of the problem. A
mystery always includes the self. I can not reflect on a mystery
without including myself within the mystery. Whenever I philosophically reflect on the meaning of death, freedom, love, being,
I necessarily am included in the reflection.

The second difference between a problem and a mystery is
similar to the first. A problem is there for anyone. It is indifferent to the person doing the reflection. Study of a problem could
be done by me or by you or by anyone. A mystery not only
includes the one doing the reflection but reflection can only be
done by the one included within the mystery. No one else can
reflect on the meaning of my death or my freedom in the way
that I can. No one can substitute for me. A mystery is always
mine and can only be reflected on by me.

A third difference between a problem and a mystery is the
mood that pervades each. When dealing with a problem the
mood is curiosity. The person struggling with a problem wants
to reach the solution. The mood in dealing with a mystery is one
of reverence, awe, wonder. I tend to think of mystery as dealing

with that which is intimately connected with the holy[3] though it certainly is not necessarily tied to any formal religion or any ecclesiastical community or church. I imagine the person dealing with mystery as dealing with something special, something precious, something that must be approached carefully and even gently.

Finally, unlike mysteries, problems have answers. If one thinker does not find the solution then it is possible that another will. With a mystery there is no answer or final solution. With a mystery a person can delve deeper and deeper but never reach the bottom. The meaning of a mystery is inexhaustible. This is not because there is so little truth in a mystery but because there is so much truth in a mystery. There is a sense in which each time you begin to reflect on a mystery you begin anew.

Because it deals with mystery, philosophy is extremely personal. Because of the nature of mystery, philosophy can not be crystal clear. This is not to say that it cannot be true, but only to call attention to the essential lack of clarity that philosophy at its best must have. I agree with Søren Kierkegaard concerning the nature of truth: that which is most personal is most true.[4] Bergman's films are mystery-laden in two senses: they deal with mystery—life, love, death—and are works of art. As works of art they are extensions of the human and so they share in the mystery that the human existent is. A book dealing with Bergman's films is a book dealing with mysteries that dramatize mysteries.

In addition to its personal nature, philosophy's angle of vision or perspective contributes to its lack of clarity. Philosophy takes the most radical stance and asks the ultimate questions. It wants to know as thoroughly and as profoundly as possible. There are many possible perspectives or angles of vision that can be assumed when an individual is engaged in an act of knowing. Let us use an example of me trying to know a dog. I can try to know the dog from the perspective of biology, from the perspective of anatomy, from the perspective of chemistry, from the perspective of physiology, from the perspective of philosophy. One perspective that I do not think I can assume is the perspective of the dog. I am human not animal. Anything I know, I know from the perspective of a human; I cannot know anything in the way that an animal knows because I am not an animal.

In trying to know the dog from the perspective of philosophy I am trying to know it in the most profound way. Philosophy wants to know the ultimate meaning of the being of the dog. Philosophy keeps asking "What *is* it?" with the emphasis on the word *is* and "What is the *meaning* of it?" with the emphasis on *meaning.* This is the perspective or angle of vision that philosophy takes on any reality that it studies.

In maintaining angles of vision and perspectives on reality we are speaking of what some philosophers have called intentionalities. An intentionality is a way of looking at something. Not only does each person take various intentionalites in knowing objects but each person has what might be called an ultimate intentionality or a vision of reality or, if you like, a faith though I do not mean to tie the word faith necessarily to a religious tradition. That ultimate intentionality is related to the person's horizon or world. By a person's horizon or world I mean to indicate the network of meanings that are real to that person. I think that some very important meanings in Bergman's horizon can become evident by viewing and reflecting on the films he created during the twenty-five year period from 1957 to 1982. Philosopher-theologian Bernard Lonergan is good on the meaning of horizon or world.

There is a sense in which it may be said that each of us lives in a world of his own. That world usually is a bounded world, and its boundary is fixed by the range of our interests and our knowledge. There are things that exist, that are known to other men, but about them I know nothing at all. There are objects of interest that concern other men, but about them I could not care less. So the extent of our knowledge and the reach of our interests fix a horizon. Within that horizon we are confined.

Such confinement may result from the historical tradition within which we are born, from the limitations of the social milieu in which we were brought up, from our individual psychological aptitudes, efforts, misadventures.[5]

Of course we are confined within a world only for a time. Events or experiences or even our own decisions can move us into a broader or deeper world or unfortunately into a less broad and less deep world. We should not think of an horizon or a world as static, fixed or finished.[6] Even though we may exist within the same horizon or world for a long time, horizon or world is by its very nature a dynamic reality. Rollo May has written:

World is the structure of meaningful relationships in which a person exists and in the design of which he participates. Thus world includes the past events which condition my existence and all the vast variety of deterministic influences which operate upon me. But it is these as I relate to them, am aware of them, carry them with me, molding, inevitably forming, building them in every minute of relating. For to be aware of one's world means at the same time to be designing it.[7]

There is a dynamic interaction between a person and his or her horizon or world. As a person changes the person's world changes, as the world changes the person changes. Of course some changes are slight and barely noticeable. I read a newspaper superficially, casually make a new acquaintance, receive a slight raise in pay, see an escapist film and none of these experiences deeply affect me or significantly alter my horizon. But if we change the examples we can see that there are encounters in which something rather important might occur. Imagine that I seriously read one of the classics, fall in love, lose my job, see a cinematic masterpiece. Now it is quite likely that my horizon dramatically changes. What happens to me because of such experiences might even be called a conversion.[8] My horizon or world might be radically changed. What I previously thought was important I may no longer think is important, what never even occurred to me as momentous previously now may assume a position of central importance in my horizon. We shall see that though Bergman's vision is strikingly consistent over the years, there is some shift in his emphasis on God from the time of *The Seventh Seal* to the filming of *Fanny and Alexander*.

Because of the process of forming and designing I like to think of a human person as dialogical, as constantly engaged in a give and take with reality. Human persons in relation to reality might be described as listeners. A person listens and tries to respond. All sorts of messages and words can be heard. Some meanings might be superficial but other meanings are mixed with mystery. The notion of person as dialogical fits in with what has been said about world or horizon. An individual achieves his or her horizon through dialogue.

This book involves dialogue in at least three ways: it is a dialogue between the author and Bergman, between the author and the reader and between Bergman, albeit filtered through the author, and the reader. Because the author figures in all three dialogues his own philosophic vision will play a crucial role in his judgments about Bergman's films. Before commenting on the philosophic vision of Bergman I think it is a good idea to put my own philosophical cards on the table. My sketch of my philosophical vision should make evident my views on God, death, art and love. I hope my articulation of my vision will encourage the reader to reflect on his or her views of God, death, art and love. If that happens the dialogue will be advanced.

I am a philosophical realist in the tradition of Aristotle and Aquinas. There is, I believe, a natural consonance between reality and the human mind. Though I hope that I have the healthy wariness and caution that should be part of any episte- mologist's makeup, especially since Immanuel Kant's Coperni- can revolution, I reject all philosophies of skepticism. Unlike Kant I think that the human mind can know reality as it is and I disagree with the genius from Konigsberg in that I deny that there is some really real which underlies appearing reality. My view is that the mind can know, however vaguely, whatever is.

In terms of my own intellectual journey and my present philo- sophical view of reality, two contemporary thought currents greatly influenced my horizon: existentialism and personalism. Some of the best known existentialists such as Jean Paul Sartre and Albert Camus were atheists, and their posing of the problem of God's existence has called me to a new philosophical under- standing of God. Philosophically, I am a theist. My view is that if the principle of sufficient reason is accepted then the existence of God can be proven. If every being must be intelligible either in itself or through another then the human mind must eventu- ally affirm the existence of a Supreme Being Who is the ultimate source of intelligibility in the universe. Though God is Mystery and we can not know *what* He is, I think we can know *that* He is.[9] To deny the reality of God is to adopt some form of absurdist position. It is to claim either that the mind cannot know reality or that reality does not make ultimate sense. Scholar John Haught summarizes the position of these philosophers clearly:

They tell us that if we honestly follow our desire for the truth we will have to admit that ultimately reality as such is either hostile or indiffer- ent to us. They point especially to the facts of suffering and death as evidence that, in the final analysis, we are not cared for. They admit that we have a powerful longing for affection and love, but they advise us to reach some compromise between the demand for acceptance and the ultimate opaqueness of "reality" to any such desire. This view may be called "absurdist" since it sees an irrational flaw at the heart of reality dividing it dualistically into two incommensurable elements: human consciousness with its desire for acceptance on the one side, and the universe with its refusal to satisfy this desire on the other. The incongruity of these two sides of reality, namely man and the universe, means that reality as a whole does not make sense. It is absurd.[10]

Such a position is a real option to anyone who wishes to choose it, but I would suggest to such persons that because they have opted for an absurdist position they should, to be consistent with their own position, live as though reality is absurd. To claim that reality is absurd and then to live as though it were meaningful is to live in a contradictory fashion. If one accepts the absurdist position one should live out the implications of that position.[11] I suggest that it is inconsistent to claim that reality does not make ultimate sense and then to live as though it does by devoting your life to serving the poor or to forming a world government or to creating works of art. All such activities implicitly suggest that there is meaning to reality and that the human project has some point. An absurdist position can not provide an adequate justification for any activity that is an effort to better the lot of the human race or to introduce more order into global affairs, or to express the dignity and beauty either of human existence or nature. All such activities for their justification demand that reality have some ultimate meaning even if that meaning is more than a little mysterious.

I think that Bergman comes close to embracing the absurdist position but he avoids it because of his views on art and love. However, a film like *Shame* is a brilliant depiction of how the world would seem to someone who endorses the absurdist position. I think the meaning of the film could be illuminated if Sartrian categories were used.

In addition to their posing of the question of God's existence in striking terms I am indebted to the existentialists for their emphasis on human freedom. The existentialists have reminded us that for better or worse persons are free.[12] From his absurdist position Sartre announced that we are condemned to be free.[13] In his plays *No Exit* and *The Flies*, Sartre dramatized the loneliness and anxiety that plagues the free person in a world without God or ultimate meaning.[14]

In contrast to Sartre's pessimistic view of freedom, a freedom that demands the nonexistence of God, I would say that we are called to be free. Human life is a journey that should lead to deeper and deeper freedom.[15] Whatever we take the meaning of human existence to be, whatever vocations we choose for ourselves, we should be concerned about the deepening and expansion of our freedom. It is our freedom along with our rational intelligence that makes us human. Any vocation we choose, or marriage partner we exchange vows with, or religion we join ought to in some significant ways deepen and expand our freedom. If this is not so we should seriously evaluate our commitments, because instead of freeing us, which is what they should do, they are working against our freedom, which is to say that they are violating our personhood.

From personalists such as Martin Buber and Emmanuel Mounier I have come to see the central role that love must play in human existence. Using Buber's basic categories of I-It and I-Thou we could evaluate contemporary interpersonal relationships. There are frightening signs that I-It relationships, that is relationships in which one person reduces the other to an object or a function perhaps to be dominated or manipulated, are on the increase. A consumer society fosters such relationships. Through I-Thou relationships in which the ineffable mystery of one person is present in reverence, concern and love to the mystery of another, people grow in their personhood.[16] My own philosophical vision is that I-Thou relations between persons and God are the ultimate purpose and meaning of human existence. The ultimate reason why human persons have been created conscious and free is so that they might enter into an I-Thou relation with one another and with God. I think that an I-Thou relationship conquers even death and so I believe that human persons are immortal.

In my own philosophy I emphasize the relational aspect of human existence. Certainly I share this preoccupation with Bergman. Borrowing from existentialists and personalists I would say that what distinguishes human existence from all other types of being in our experience is the human being's capacity to relate consciously.[17] This distinguishing aspect of human existence might be described as "openness to other," as "presence to other." The word *existence* actually captures the idea. The word *existence* suggests that a person puts himself outside himself.[18] To be person is to be that type of being who stands outside himself or herself in conscious bodiliness.

Reacting against all forms of spiritualism and angelism that denigrate the human body, I would stress the importance of the human body in all human activity whether the activity be as mundane as eating or as exalted as contemplation and prayer. This is why I think that Bergman is onto something very important when in films such as *Winter Light* (1963) or *The Silence* (1963) or *The Touch* (1971) he emphasizes the importance of touch and uses touch as a sign and metaphor for love. If I had to choose between two alternative descriptions of the relationship between myself and my body, "I have a body" or "I am a body," I would opt for the latter, even though it is not an adequate articulation of the being of human bodiliness. The human body is unlike every other type of body.[19] It participates in subjectivity or selfhood. It is not only our minds that are conscious. Our bodies are conscious and open us out to relationships with what we encounter in our experience. We are "incarnate spirits." To miss the truth about ourselves is to miss the mystery each of us is.[20]

My philosophy of personal existence stresses the central role of love in interpersonal relationships. I agree completely with the statement of the mystic St. John of the Cross "In the evening of our lives we shall be judged on how we have loved." Not only do I benefit those whom I love but I grow enormously through the activity of loving. Every free choice can enhance and enrich my existence but no free choice so enriches the existence of the person as the free choice to love. Loving and being loved are the two most important human experiences. As a generalization we can say that we are more capable of loving to the extent that we have received love. Philosopher Frederick Wilhelmsen's description of being loved is accurate: "What being-*loved* makes being do is precisely *be*."[21] We shall see that for Bergman interpersonal human love is the only salvation available.

Not only is the experience of loving and being loved extremely important in human interpersonal relationships but I think that the love relationship between human persons and God reveals the most basic truth about human existence and divine existence. Unfortunately the word "God" for many contemporary people has bad connotations. It does but it need not. Without referring to the view of God presented by any religion we can still note two very important philosophical truths about God. Because God is the source of all truth and all good, whenever I know anything I implicitly know God and whenever I love any good I implicitly love God. The horizon or background against which all truth and goodness appear is divine. So the relational nature of human existence is a radical openness to the divine. To know and love God directly and consciously is to make explicit what is implicit in all human knowing and loving.

In my philosophical vision art plays a very important role. No person's horizon is ever fixed or finished. There is, as long as there is life, a dynamic relationship between the person and his or her horizon. The experience of great art can deepen and broaden a person's horizon or world. The great artist makes an enormously important contribution to people.

For my views on art I am greatly indebted to the writings of philosopher Jacques Maritain;[22] for my views on film to the "Aristotle of the Cinema," Andre Bazin.[23] We can look at art as a human activity or as a product of a human activity. If we consider art as a human activity then art is a virtue, that is, a habit achieved through repeated actions, of knowing how to make something. The shoemaker or the sculptor has the virtue of art in a way that I do not: I don't know how to make a shoe or carve a statue in stone. If we look at art as a product then the important distinction between servile art and fine art can be seen clearly. A servile work of art is made for some practical use. For example, a shoe is for walking. A work of fine art is made for itself, *ars gratia artis*. A statue, for instance, is not for use but only to be viewed. If the shoe does the job that a shoe should do we might say that the shoemaker is a skilled artist. If the statue is especially striking or beautiful we might say that the sculptor is a skilled artist. A work of fine art, at least in some way, reveals beauty. You do not use a work of fine art, you just experience it and depending on how beautiful it is it can affect you profoundly.

In a work of fine art the two key ingredients are the skill of the artist and the creative intuition that inspires his work. In a work of servile art the artist produces in order to fulfill some need, e.g., shoes, eating utensils, clothes, automobiles. In the work of fine art the artist wishes to express something, incarnate something in the particular piece of art. What is required for the artist to produce the work of fine art is creative intuition and the skill or expertise to express that creative intuition in an external work.

It is possible that a person may have creative intuition and yet not have the virtue of art and so not know how to incarnate that creative intuition. It is also possible that someone has enormous skill in making things but not have any creative intuition and so what he or she produces is not especially striking. In the great works of art we have a wedding of a creative intuition and a marvelous expression of that creative intuition in stone or on canvas or in music or whatever medium the artist uses to express the intuition.

In relation to a person's horizon it is impossible to overestimate the importance of great art. Because it leads us more deeply into the human mystery, a great work of art can significantly influence our dialogue with reality and in important ways deepen and expand our horizons. Ingmar Bergman has made films that are genuine masterpieces. With exceptional skill and apparently with an extraordinary relationship with his fellow artists Bergman has been able to express his creative intuition on celluloid. About creative intuition Bergman said:

A film for me begins with something very vague—a chance remark or a bit of conversation, a hazy but agreeable event unrelated to any particular situation. It can be a few bars of music, a shaft of light across the street. Sometimes in my work at the theater I have envisioned actors made up for yet unplayed roles.

These are split-second impressions that disappear as quickly as they come, yet leave behind a mood—like pleasant dreams. It is a mental state, not an actual story, but one abounding in fertile associations and images. Most of all, it is a brightly colored thread sticking out of the dark sack of the unconscious. If I begin to wind up this thread, and do it carefully, a complete film will emerge.[24]

In another interview in which he was discussing his method of writing a film he said:

I'll try to be as concrete as I can. While I'm writing, I'm immune to all
marginal discussion. It hardly exists at all. If it did, I think I'd fall into
such despondency, such a feeling of exposing myself and others, that
I'd simply cancel the whole production out of sheer bashfulness. Actors get their teeth into it at quite another level. From their theatre
work they're used to getting to grips with an author and a role and to
asking themselves: "What's really behind this, why has he written this
or that?" They come up and say things which can be painful, and often
one shies away and says: "That's not how it is at all, that's not right."
But secretly one often has to agree with them. All the time a film is
being made, one flinches away from marginal thinking. If I rely on my
intuition I know it will lead me in the right direction. I don't need to
argue with it. If I begin hesitating and discussing, I get so tangled up in
personal complications and become so crudely aware of what it really is
I'm depicting, I can't go on. Afterwards, I can often realize what I've
really made, what I've depicted, or written.[25]

Of course the creative intuition is accessible to us only in the
finished work of art. If Bergman could articulate in a sentence or
two what his creative intuition is he would have no need to create
a work of art. If we wish to experience the intuition at the heart
of a Bergman film then we must see the film. More than any
other director's body of work Bergman's corpus of film can
provide for us what James Joyce has described as aesthetic
pleasure:

The instant wherein that supreme quality of beauty, the clear radiance
of the esthetic image, is apprehended luminously by the mind which
has been arrested by its wholeness and fascinated by its harmony is the
luminous silent stasis of esthetic pleasure. . .[26]

What I am trying to do in this book is articulate the philosophy
that is present in a large number of Bergman films. I am con-

cerned that I not articulate a philosophy of screenplay; I am interested in the vision that underlies the finished works and that vision, though it includes the story, also includes everything else that goes to make up the creative work such as camera angles, lighting, color, sound, music and so forth.

I am also concerned that I tell you not what *I* took from the films but what the films objectively contain. This is not a book about *my* reactions to Bergman's films but about Bergman's films. Years ago Arthur Gibson wrote an exceptionally provocative book using seven of Bergman's films: *The Silence of God: Creative Response to the Films of Ingmar Bergman.*[27] The author was not so interested in interpreting Bergman's films as creatively responding to them. Gibson claimed that he was trying neither to provide an adequate interpretation of Bergman's films nor to twist Bergman's films to fit a meaning that Gibson had thought up. Rather, Gibson wished to report to his readers the reactions, thoughts and insights that he had from encountering the images that Bergman had put up on the screen. That Gibson's reflections are so exciting reveal how much can be "taken" from a Bergman film.[28] My goal is different from Gibson's. Rather than offer a creative response, I am trying to articulate the philosophical vision that the films offer. Gibson might admit that the source of much of his response is Gibson as much as it is Bergman. I would not make a similar admission of my discussion of Bergman. The bulk of this book is about Bergman's philosophical vision, not Lauder's. In this chapter I have articulated my own philosophical vision in order that the reader knows the author's outlook and also to encourage the reader to reflect on his or her philosophical vision. I disagree with Bergman on God, death, art and love but I am deeply grateful for his profound dramatic treatments of these topics. Enough about me. Let us turn toward cinema's greatest single talent.

2

The Artist as Contemporary Spokesperson

SIMILAR IN SOME WAYS to plays, cinema is a fine art. Many artists contribute to the making of a film—writers, actors, lighting crew, makeup, composers, musicians, set designers, directors. Any one of these artists can make a significant contribution to the finished film, or do such a poor job that the film's value as a work of art suffers considerably. If there is one artist to whom the finished product can be attributed more than to any other, that artist is the director. More than any other artist the director must take responsibility for the success or failure of the film as a work of art. It is the director who must join together the various talents that contribute to a film and weave their offerings together into the finished product.

Author/director Bergman is most responsible for any philosophical meaning that his films convey. However, in looking to Bergman for philosophy, some caution is required. Bruce F. Kawin made the following comment in discussing Bergman:

Even to make a film as conceptually intricate as *Persona* is largely a matter of storytelling, not of philosophizing. If any ideas emerge from Bergman's stories, they do so because they are elemental to his emotional imagination—because they are part of the way he sees human relationships. His works do not set out to propound theses, yet because their imagery is rich and their characters are often able to put their tensions into words, these films are uncommonly suggestive, both emotionally and intellectually.[1]

Kawin is correct in emphasizing that Bergman is not a professional philosopher but a storyteller. But of course the way that someone "sees human relationships" is very much a part of that person's philosophic vision. In his book on Bergman Vernon Young makes a point about Bergman similar to that made by Kawin:

He is not an intellectual, he is an artist, that is to say, a maker of expressive forms. Initially he responds to images, provocations and fugitive visions. Thereafter he proceeds from creative intuition and personal bias, reacting to experience subjectively (not to say obsessively), selecting from phenomena those elements which alone can feed his immediate artistic purpose. A muddled interpretation of what constitutes intellectual expression must be responsible for supposing that because Bergman's best films appeal to our minds as well as to our emotions, a rare consummation in the cinema, they were therefore intellectually conceived. Art may comprise a degree of intellectual activity, but it is not a synonym for intellectual activity.[2]

While it is true that Bergman is primarily an artist his art incarnates a very strong and, I believe, philosophically consistent vision. Speaking of his fellow-artist, film director Jean-Luc Godard said "for Bergman, to be alone means to ask questions. And to make films means to answer them."[3] The questions that Bergman asks are philosophical questions and so his films are a marriage of movies and metaphysics. My insistence that Bergman's films are filled with philosophy might be more clear if we recall what philosophy is. From the time that the pre-Socratics Thales, Anaximander and Anaximenes confronted reality with questions concerning its ultimate makeup, philosophy has been characterized as asking ultimate questions. Philosophy is never satisfied with descriptions or reports. Mere appearances cannot quell its hunger. Philosophy wants to dig as deeply as the human mind can probe and discover the meaning of life, death, God, freedom, love and indeed of knowledge itself. Check any of Plato's *Dialogues* and you will see philosophy incarnated in the person of Socrates searching for answers. See any Bergman film and you will have an analogous experience. What distinguishes Bergman from the rest of us in our philosophical search is that he dramatizes his questions and answers on film. Before he began to shoot *Face to Face* Bergman wrote his fellow workers a letter discussing their new project. He wrote:

We're now going to make a film which, in a way, is about an attempted suicide. Actually it deals ("as usual" I was about to say!) with Life, Love, and Death. Because nothing in fact is more important. To occupy oneself with. To think of. To worry over. To be happy about. And so on.[4]

In talking about a film that "as usual" will deal with "Life, Love and Death" Bergman is in effect articulating a paraphrase of the title of this book. Bergman the artist probes deeply into dimensions of the real.[5] With enormous skill Bergman filters his philosophy through film and his audience has an opportunity to experience in dramatic form the questions that preoccupy philosophers: Is there a God? Can we be certain there is? If there is, why is God silent? What can we know? Can we love? What is death? Bergman, in discussing his vocation as filmmaker and his lifelong fascination with film has said:

I have often wondered what fascinates me and still fascinates me in the same way. Something can occur to me in the studio, or in the darkness of the editing room when I have the small frame in front of me and the film strip running through my fingers, or during the fantastic birth process of mixing when the finished film slowly unveils its face. It is a thought that I cannot resist; namely, that I work with a medium so refined that it should be able to illuminate the human soul far more sharply, reveal still more ruthlessly and corner completely new areas of reality for our knowledge. Perhaps we might even find a crack to penetrate to the twilight land of surreality, told in a new and revolutionizing way.[6]

Bergman is fond of quoting Eugene O'Neill's statement, "Drama that doesn't deal with man's relation to God is worthless," and he has been misinterpreted as meaning that all film must deal with specifically religious themes. In trying to clarify what he means in using the O'Neill quote Bergman stated:

Yes, and I've often quoted him, and been thoroughly misunderstood. Today we say all art is political. But I'd say all art has to do with ethics. Which after all really comes to the same thing. It's a matter of attitudes. That's what O'Neill meant.[7]

What Bergman means by "ethics" is what preoccupies the philosopher. O'Neill and Bergman mean that art must deal with the ultimate questions. At least once in discussing his own philosophical vision Bergman articulated a position that might be interpreted as behavioristic or deterministic.[8] An argument might be made that in the film *From the Life of the Marionettes* (1980) the characters are totally subject to forces beyond their control and are not really free. However any evidence from that film supporting an interpretation of Bergman's philosophical vision as behavioristic or deterministic would be outweighed by the numerous films that Bergman made depicting persons who, though influenced by internal and external forces, are freely struggling to become more free and especially more loving. If Bergman's vision of human beings was that they are totally determined, his emphasis on the value of love would be pointless.

An overview of the films that Ingmar Bergman created during the twenty-five year period from *The Seventh Seal* (1957) to *Fanny and Alexander* (1982) presents a strikingly unified vision. Almost any film could be chosen to illustrate the philosophical vision that emerges from Bergman's cinematic output concerning God or death or art or love, so consistent were Bergman's preoccupations during this period. Of course a particular topic is more thoroughly treated in a particular film, such as God in *Winter Light* or death in *Cries and Whispers* (1973) or art in *Persona* (1966) or love in *The Touch*, but that does not mean that there is not some reference to all four topics in each film. What Bergman has presented in his films have been his consistent preoccupations throughout his career. Bergman has said:

The people in my films are exactly like myself—creatures of instinct, or rather poor intellectual capacity, who at best only think while they're talking. Mostly they're body, with a little hollow for the soul. My films draw on my own experience; however inadequately based logically and intellectually.[9]

Even Bergman's film career of writing and directing prior to *The Seventh Seal* reveals his interest in the four topics I have chosen to summarize his vision, but that vision does not come across as powerfully in those early films as it does once the author/director began to work at the height of his creative powers. Dealing with familiar Bergman themes, *Close to Life* (1958) and *The Devil's Eye* (1960) in terms of their artistic merit seem to fit better with the films that preceded *The Seventh Seal* than with some of the masterpieces that followed it.

It is important that we do not reduce Bergman to a preacher

promoting a gospel or even a pedant peddling a *Weltanschauung*. When asked whether he has ever felt himself to be some sort of a religious preacher or a prophet Bergman replied "Certainly not! For me things have always been on the one hand, it's like this— but on the other, like that!"[10] In discussing the philosophic vision of Bergman I do not wish to give the impression that he has decided to teach his audience through the medium of film what he takes to be the ultimate meaning of God, death, art and love. Bergman is an artist, not an instructor. However, it is inevitable that when an artist probes his own experience as deeply as Bergman does, more than a little of the creator is revealed in the creation. In his book in which he discusses several film directors, Roy Armes says that in looking at the artist figures in some of Bergman's films "we are faced with an almost indecent sense of direct communication with a creator who has stripped himself morally and emotionally naked."[11] In an extraordinarily perceptive essay on Bergman's biographical background Birgitta Steene claims that Bergman is very much in touch with his childhood experiences. Bergman has confessed:

When I am about to fall asleep in the evening or about to take my afternoon nap or relax a little and I find myself in a state between dreaming and waking, which is a rather spellbinding state, I can suddenly and without any difficulty call forth memories from my early childhood: lights, smells, voices, movements, lines that people spoke which still seem enormously secretive to me and quite unfathomable, exactly as they did when I was a child.[12]

Steene claims that there are two different milieus in Bergman's early life that provide the emotional and thematic core of his films.[13] One looks to his grandmother's apartment and his earliest childhood memories, a world of another time and life-style that was sensuous and magic; the other is his parents' home which Bergman recalls as stern, authoritative and moralistic. Steene suggests that generally speaking Bergman's films came from the authoritative world. She writes:

The person who reveals the skeletons in the closet is the little boy Ingmar turned filmmaker. The darkroom of the film processing becomes both a metaphor for the dark recesses of the mind, journeying back into the childhood past, and an act of exorcism through which the frightening shadows of early traumas are dispelled. The therapeutic aspect of the creative process is not entirely successful, however; hence his return to the same motifs in film after film. The silence that his parents used as punishment for disobedience swells into the taunting, silent, and monstrous god-figure of the metaphysical films. The traumatic incident when the child Ingmar was locked in the dark closet and told that a nasty goblin lived there who fed on the toes of little children, recurs in both *Hour of the Wolf* and *Face to Face*, and is alluded to in *A Passion* and *Shame*.[14]

Steene's account would be supported by a reading of Bergman's autobiography. It is difficult not to admire Bergman's honesty in painting his self-portrait, and anyone interested in reading a genius' report on his life should find the autobiography interesting. However the light that the book sheds on the philosophy in Bergman's films is at best indirect. Though there are interesting anecdotes and confessions of artistic failures Bergman does not discuss the themes of his films either in detail or in depth. What does emerge from the book is the portrait of an extremely sensitive artist who creates from the depths of his personal preoccupations. Perhaps a psychologist could use the autobiography and Bergman's films to construct a psychohistory of the artist. We will focus more directly on the themes in the films.

While I will avoid identifying any individual characters in any

films with Bergman it seems clear that there have been performers that Bergman considered especially apt to convey his deepest
feelings. For example, Bergman, who seems to have an especially close relationship with the artists who work with him, did
suggest that Max von Sydow has played a special part in his
films.[16] Steene is correct in suggesting that in some films Bergman uses women to dramatize his deepest feelings,[17] and I think
that in more than one film Liv Ullmann becomes like an alter
ego in that the characters she portrays reveal some of Bergman's
deepest feelings.[18] However, what I am most interested in is not
which character in which film most resembles Bergman and in
what way, but rather what philosophical vision is evident in
Bergman's most important films over a twenty-five year period.

A work that can be used as a paradigm for all the important
themes that have preoccupied Bergman throughout his film
career is *The Seventh Seal*. It has been noted that among Bergman's films "it is the one that perhaps most exactly formulates
something of a philosophical credo."[19] I think I have seen the
film eight or nine times but I can still recall the thrill of seeing it
for the first time approximately thirty years ago. The film, which
takes its title from the Book of Revelation, was a revelation to me
of what could be done on a movie screen. Then, and I must say
even now, the film seemed like a lovely poem, a poem that had its
flashes of terror and bleakness but one that basically affirmed
the human mystery in however tentative terms.

In this highly allegorical film[20] Bergman tells the story of a
knight (Max von Sydow) battling with Death (Bengt Ekerot).
The title of the film is from Chapter 8, v. 1 of the Book of
Revelation: "The Lamb then broke the seventh seal, and there
was silence in heaven for about half an hour." In the book the
pause seems to be a period of silence to underscore the solemn
moment that precedes the coming of God.[21] For Bergman the
half hour of silence is the opportunity for a moment of truth, an

interruption that gives us time to reflect philosophically and try to make sense of human existence. The film is the artistic expression of Bergman's philosophical response. Here is an allegory that raises most important questions about God, death, art and love and presents some possible responses. The film is Bergman's response to the silence in heaven.

The opening shots of *The Seventh Seal* set the scene for the philosophical probing of its main character, Antonius Bloch, a medieval knight. The film begins with the singing of a church choir on the sound track. The singing stops abruptly and there is complete silence. The camera reveals the knight who is waking up and his squire, Jons, who lies asleep. They are resting on their journey home after ten years of disillusioning experience in the Crusades. A plague is ravaging the land. The time is early morning and the light is gray. As Birgitta Steene suggests "nature seems to lie in a coma."[22] The visuals in the opening shots place us in what can be described as the mythic country of death.[23] After the knight says his morning prayers Death appears to him and announces that the time for the knight's departure from this life has arrived. The knight suggests that his death be delayed while he and Death play a game of chess. The shot of Death and the knight sitting to play chess on a hillside against a darkened but beautiful background of sea and sky is one that is quintessential Bergman. This shot, as do others in Bergman films, sums up not only this film but much of Bergman's work. The human person is trying to find some meaning in the face of death. Bergman's creation of a film, a work of art, indicates something of the meaning he has found.

Though the time setting of *The Seventh Seal* is medieval the intellectual setting is contemporary. Bergman, noting that the medieval world depicted in the film is an historical metaphor for the contemporary world threatened by an atomic bomb, said:

Death (Bengt Ekerot) beckoning to the Knight (Max von Sydow).

In my film the crusader returns from the Crusades as the soldier returns from the war today. In the Middle Ages, men lived in terror of the plague. Today they live in terror of the atomic bomb. *The Seventh Seal* is an allegory with a theme that is quite simple: man, his eternal search for God, with death as his only certainty.[24]

The knight and his squire serve as a counterpoint throughout the film: the knight is earnest in his search for God and will never give up his search for ultimate knowledge; the squire is a skeptic whose interests are totally terrestrial. Though the knight is preoccupied with questions about God, the squire expresses his own philosophy succinctly at one point in the film. The scene is the exceptionally striking one in which a procession of penitents scourging themselves and being led by monks, pass by the inn at which the knight and squire have stopped. One of the monks gives a brief sermon about how the plague is a scourge from God. Squire Jons says:

This damned ranting about doom. Is that food for the minds of modern people? Do they really expect us to take them seriously?

After the knight smiles tiredly the squire continues:

Yes, now you grin at me, my lord. But allow me to point out that I've either read, heard or experienced most of the tales which we people tell each other. Even the ghost stories about God the Father, the angels, Jesus Christ and the Holy Ghost—all these I've accepted without too much emotion. My little stomach is my world, my head is my eternity, and my hands, two wonderful suns. My legs are time's damned pendulums, and my dirty feet are two splendid starting points for my philosophy. Everything is worth precisely as much as a belch, the only difference being that a belch is more satisfying.[25]

As the knight and squire continue their journey toward home, Death from time to time appears to the knight and they continue their game of chess. During the journey home the knight meets various characters and both these and the experiences that he undergoes provide a setting in which Bergman touches on his favorite themes.

The knight meets an acting troupe made up of a juggler Jof (Nils Poppe), his wife Mia (Bibi Andersson), their business manager and fellow actor Skat (Erik Strandmark). Jof and Mia have their baby son Michael with them. At one point in the film Jof, who claims to have visions of the Blessed Mother, announces that some day his son will perform the impossible trick: he will throw a ball into the air and suspend it there. Reference to this trick, their names, their beautiful love for one another and their escape from Death which comes about indirectly because of their love make it clear that the couple and their child function as some type of symbol of the Holy Family.[26] In a crucial scene in the film the knight, who has been terribly discouraged by the pointlessness of the savagery and plundering that characterized the crusades, by the plague that has been taking so many lives and by his inability to find some significant meaning in life during the pauses in the chess game with Death, sits on a hillside with Jof and Mia and their child. The scene is exceptionally beautiful.[27] The knight is initially terribly disturbed by the questions that have preoccupied him. He says to Mia:

Faith is a torment, did you know that? It is like loving someone who is out there in the darkness but never appears, no matter how loudly you call.

When Mia says that she does not understand the knight replies:

Jof (Nils Poppe) telling Mia (Bibi Andersson) about his vision of the Blessed Virgin and Child.

Everything I've said seems meaningless and unreal while I sit here with you and your husband. How unimportant it all becomes suddenly.[28]

Observing the love within the family, the knight holding in his hands a bowl of milk and strawberries given to him by Jof and Mia says:

I shall remember this moment. The silence, the twilight, the bowls of strawberries and milk, your faces in the evening light. Michael sleeping, Jof with his lyre. I'll try to remember what we have talked about. I'll carry this memory between my hands as carefully as if it were a bowl filled to the brim with fresh milk. And it will be an adequate sign—it will be enough for me.[29]

In Bergman's world, milk and strawberries are symbols of love, a kind of Eucharist symbolizing communion between human beings.[30] The knight holds the milk and strawberries as a priest might elevate the sacred species at a Mass. In this scene and in the presence of the characters of Jof and Mia in the film, we can see two preoccupations of Bergman that reappear in film after film. The first is the importance of love. Bergman has said, "Whenever I am in doubt or uncertainty I take refuge in the vision of a simple and pure love."[31] The second is the role of religion and specifically the Christian religion and Christian symbols in the world. It is Bergman's view of religion and Christian symbols as much as anything else which makes him unique among contemporary film artists. As we will see in the chapter on God, at times Christian symbols are used to highlight the presence of love; at times they are used to underline the absence of love.

On his journey the knight also meets Plog the smith (Ake Fridell) and his wife Lisa (Inga Gill) who has an affair with Skat. The strains and stresses of heterosexual relationships are lightly and humorously treated in this film. But in almost every other Bergman film they will be depicted with such seriousness, insight, honesty and integrity that for some viewers a Bergman film becomes almost unbearable. What film can match *Scenes from a Marriage* in its depiction, albeit one-sided, of the difficulties and strains of married life?

The knight also meets Raval (Bertil Anderberg), a seminarian, who is one of the most unattractive characters in any Bergman film. A liar, cheat and bully, he, along with other references in *The Seventh Seal,* can suggest the impotence of institutional religion. When he is stricken by the plague his death is as miserable as his life.

In contrast the death of the actor, Skat, is depicted by Bergman with a light and amusing touch. Yet a point is made about artists that reappears time and again in Bergman films: the blown up self-importance of the artist, his deception of others and perhaps even his deception of himself. The scene of Skat's death is quite humorous. Having feigned death in order to avoid a battle with Plog with whose wife he had an affair, Skat has climbed up a tree in order to hide himself until dark. Suddenly he sees that the tree on which he is sitting is being cut down by Death. When he recognizes Death, Skat pleads with him but to no advantage.

SKAT: It won't do. I haven't got time.
DEATH: So you haven't got time.
SKAT: No, I have my performance.
DEATH: Then it's been cancelled because of death.
SKAT: My contract.
DEATH: Your contract is terminated.
SKAT: My children, my family.
DEATH: Shame on you, Skat!
SKAT: Yes, I'm ashamed.

SKAT: Isn't there any way to get off?

DEATH: No, not in this case.

SKAT: No loopholes, no exceptions?. . . Perhaps you'll take a bribe. . .Help![32]

While Bergman treats the artist's role in society in a humorous way in this scene, he deals with it much more seriously in other films. At least at one point in his life Bergman seems to have had a dismal view of his own vocation.[33] There is a scene earlier in *The Seventh Seal* in which an artist seems to articulate Bergman's musings on the role of the artist in society. The knight and squire stop at a church. As the knight goes to confession the squire talks with the artist in the back of the church who is painting a rather frightening picture he calls the Dance of Death.

JONS: What is this supposed to represent?

PAINTER: The Dance of Death.

JONS: And that one is Death?

PAINTER: Yes, he dances off with all of them.

JONS: Why do you paint such nonsense?

PAINTER: I thought it would serve to remind people that they must die.

JONS: Well, it's not going to make them feel any happier.

PAINTER: Why should one always make people happy? It might not be a bad idea to scare them a little once in a while.

JONS: Then they'll close their eyes and refuse to look at your painting.

PAINTER: Oh, they'll look. A skull is almost more interesting than a naked woman.

JONS: If you do scare them . . .

PAINTER: They'll think.

JONS: And if they think. . .

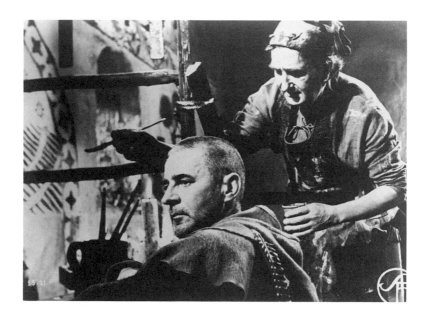

Squire (Gunnar Björnstrand) looking at the painting by the artist (Gunnar Olsson) who in his work does not hesitate to frighten people.

PAINTER: They'll become still more scared.

JONS: And then they'll run right into the arms of the priests.

PAINTER: That's not my business.

JONS: You're only painting your Dance of Death.

PAINTER: I'm only painting things as they are. Everyone else can do as he likes.

JONS: Just think how some people will curse you.

PAINTER: Maybe. But then I'll paint something amusing for them to look at. I have to make a living—at least until the plague takes me.[34]

There is another scene in which Bergman seems to be dramatizing the ambiguous role of the artist in our society. The performance by Jof, Mia and Skat is interrupted by the flagellants passing by. The villagers and Jof, bothered by the procession, gather at an inn (called "The Inn of Humiliation" in the script)[35] and then Jof is accosted by Raval. The seminarian forces the actor at knifepoint to get up on one of the tables and to act like a bear. Moments earlier the actor was an object of adulation. Now he is being humiliated. Somehow he becomes a scapegoat to be blamed not only for the seduction of the blacksmith's wife but even for the presence of the plague.[36] In many primitive societies a bear was honored by a community and eventually put to death in a sacred ritual. Jof, the artist, resembles the sacred animal and is made to play the role of victim.[37] According to Bergman, the artist in contemporary society has the terrible burden of creating in a world that has lost the ultimate meaning that it once had from religion.

One of the more frightening scenes in *The Seventh Seal* is the one in which the knight comes upon a 14-year-old girl who is being burned at the stake because she is thought to be a witch in league with the devil. The knight looks into the young girl's eyes hoping to meet the devil so that he can ask him about God.

Jof being ridiculed and intimidated by Raval (Bertil Anderberg) who
is in left background of the photo.

Looking into the eyes of the girl so near death the knight hopes to be able to discover some important meaning that has thus far escaped him. He finds nothing. As the girl is being burned at the stake Bergman has the knight and the squire in closeup staring at her engage in the following dialogue:

JONS: What does she see? Can you tell me?

KNIGHT (shakes his head): She feels no more pain.

JONS: You don't answer my question. Who watches over that child? Is it the angels, or God, or the Devil, or only the emptiness? Emptiness, my lord!

KNIGHT: This cannot be.

JONS: Look at her eyes, my lord. Her poor brain has just made a discovery. Emptiness under the moon.

KNIGHT: No.

JONS: We stand powerless, our arms hanging at our sides, because we see what she sees, and our terror and hers are the same. (an outburst) That poor little child. I can't stand it, I can't stand it. . .[38]

It is the knight's periodic meetings with Death that call us back to the central motif of the film. Except for the initial meeting on the hillside when the chess game is begun the most visually striking encounter between the two protagonists is the scene in which the knight tries to receive the Sacrament of Confession and eventually discovers that the confessor is Death. The scene is not only visually striking and illuminative—the closeup of Death's face is quite frightening and the shot composed of the knight's face and the face of Death through the grille suggests the barrier to understanding that the knight experiences as he grapples with Death—but it zeroes in on the basic questions of the film and of all of Bergman's work. The following dialogue may be as good a summary of Bergman's preoccupations as we find in any dialogue in any Bergman film. In the following dialogue the knight does not yet know that the confessor is Death.

KNIGHT: Is it so cruelly inconceivable to grasp God with the senses? Why should he hide himself in a mist of half-spoken promises and unseen miracles?

(Death doesn't answer.)

KNIGHT: How can we have faith in those who believe when we can't have faith in ourselves? What is going to happen to those of us who want to believe but aren't able to? And what is to become of those who neither want nor are capable of believing?

(The knight stops and waits for a reply, but no one speaks or answers him. There is complete silence.)

KNIGHT: Why can't I kill God within me? Why does he live on in this painful and humiliating way even though I curse Him and want to tear Him out of my heart? Why in spite of everything, is He a baffling reality that I can't shake off? Do you hear me?

DEATH: Yes, I hear you.

KNIGHT: I want knowledge, not faith, not suppositions, but knowledge. I want God to stretch out his hand toward me, reveal Himself and speak to me.

DEATH: But he remains silent.

KNIGHT: I call out to him in the dark but no one seems to be there.

DEATH: Perhaps no one is there.

KNIGHT: Then life is an outrageous horror. No one can live in the face of death, knowing that all is nothingness.

DEATH: Most people never reflect about either death or the futility of life.

KNIGHT: But one day they will have to stand at the last moment of life and look toward the darkness. . . .[39]

The Knight making his confession to Death.

Then the knight says that he is playing chess with Death and that he will use whatever time remains of his life "for one meaningful deed." When the knight realizes that it is Death to whom he has been confessing he is furious that he has been tricked. But when Death leaves, for one moment the knight seems to identify with the kind of existentialist live-for-the-moment philosophy that characterizes Jons' approach to life. The knight raises his hand, looks at it and affirms the present moment, whatever it might mean, by saying with intensity "This is my hand. I can move it, feel the blood pulsing through it. The sun is still high in the sky and I, Antonius Bloch, am playing chess with Death."[40]

Eventually the knight does perform the one meaningful deed: he deliberately distracts Death during the chess match so that Jof and Mia with their baby Michael can escape. That Jof and Mia and their baby survive is significant in the context of the film because of their love for one another.

When the knight finally arrives home to be reunited with his wife he has with him, in addition to Jons, the blacksmith and his wife, and another young woman whom Jons has saved from being raped by Raval. The six people sit down for a meal and the knight's wife reads from the section of Revelation from which the title of the film has been taken. Birgitta Steene sees the meal as a last supper without any sacramental signs of redemption.[41] Death arrives to take the six people with him. Each person remains totally within character as he or she confronts Death, e.g., the knight is praying for insight, the squire is affirming physical experience, the blacksmith and his wife confess their humanity and that they are no better or worse than most people. The final prayer of the knight and the final "mock prayer" of Jons convey two diametrically opposed views of God:

The Knight distracts Death so that Jof and Mia in background can escape with their child.

KNIGHT: From our darkness, we call out to Thee, Lord. Have mercy on us because we are small and frightened and ignorant.

JONS (bitterly): In the darkness where You are supposed to be, where all of us probably are . . . In the darkness You will find no one to listen to Your cries or be touched by Your sufferings. Wash Your tears and mirror Yourself in Your indifference.

KNIGHT: God, You who are somewhere, who must be somewhere, have mercy upon us.[42]

But the film does not end with this scene. Bergman cuts to Jof, Mia and Michael who are continuing their journey. Jof has a vision of his former companions with Death. Those who have died are urged into a dance by Death. Jof says "They dance away from the dawn and it's a solemn dance toward the dark lands, while the rain washes their faces and cleans the salt of the tears from their cheeks."[43]

The last seconds of the film are touching, and that Jof, Mia and Michael have escaped provides some sign of hope.

Much of the thematic material in *The Seventh Seal* will reappear again and again in Bergman films. The image that best characterizes a Bergman hero or heroine is a person searching for meaning. Like the knight a Bergman protagonist is never home but either journeying or residing in a place that somehow conveys isolation. These metaphors of journey-isolation are used very often by Bergman. One thinks of Dr. Isak (Victor Sjöström) in *Wild Strawberries* (1957) who is traveling to receive an honorary degree, of Albert Vogler (Max von Sydow) in *The Magician* (1958) traveling toward the capital city, of Karin (Harriet Andersson) and David (Gunnar Björnstrand) and Minus (Lars Passgard) and Martin (Max von Sydow) on an island in *Through a Glass Darkly* (1961), of Pastor Tomas (Gunnar Björnstrand) traveling from one church to another in *Winter Light* (1963), of the two sisters Ester (Ingrid Thulin) and

Opening scene of David (Gunnar Björnstrand), Karin (Harriet Andersson), Minus (Lars Passgard) and Martin (Max von Sydow) returning to island after a swim.

Anna (Gunnel Lindblom) traveling and pausing in a foreign city in *The Silence* (1963), of actress Elizabeth Vogler (Liv Ullmann) and nurse Alma (Bibi Andersson) staying at someone else's summer home in *Persona* (1966), of the acting troupe being detained in a foreign country in *The Rite* (1969), of David (Elliot Gould) visiting Sweden in *The Touch* (1970), of psychiatrist Jenny Isaksen (Liv Ullmann) summering at her grandparents' home in *Face to Face* (1976), of American Abel Rosenberg (David Carradine) in Germany and unable to speak German in *The Serpent's Egg* (1977), of concert pianist Charlotte (Ingrid Bergman) visiting her daughter's home in *Autumn Sonata* (1978). Significantly only Bergman's last film *Fanny and Alexander* (1982) seems centered on a happy home.

So from *The Seventh Seal* we have noticed the following preoccupations of Bergman: (1) the silence and perhaps absence or even nonexistence of God, (2) the necessity of confronting death in any attempt at making sense of life, (3) the vocation of the artist, sometimes adored by society and sometimes attacked, (4) the importance of love in human relationships and the frequent frustrations of heterosexual love. The cinematic expression of each of these preoccupations so develops from *The Seventh Seal* to *Fanny and Alexander* that a coherent vision of God, death, art and love becomes evident.

3

God: From Transcendent to Immanent

THERE PROBABLY IS no film author/director whose image is so connected with questions concerning the existence of God as Ingmar Bergman. Robert Bresson's films are explorations of the mystery of God's grace and human freedom, and therefore the French director's films can be described as more God-centered[1] than Bergman's. But in Bresson's films God is an implied presence, not a problem. In Bergman's films God is either a question, or a silence, or a "spider," or an absence whose previous presence is only recalled through religious symbols that now have a thoroughly immanent meaning. The journey of God from the center of Bergman's preoccupations to the fringes of the Swedish director's artistic consciousness is not difficult to chart. Bergman has said:

As the religious aspect of my existence was wiped out, life became much easier to live. Sartre has said how inhibited he used to be as an artist and author, how he suffered because what he was doing wasn't good enough. By a slow intellectual process he came to realize that his anxieties about not making anything of value were an atavistic relic from the religious notion that something exists which can be called the Supreme Good, or that anything is perfect. When he'd dug up this secret idea, this relic, had seen through it and amputated it, he lost his artistic inhibitions too.

Pastor Tomas (Gunnar Björnstrand) struggles with the silence of
God.

I've been through something very similar. When my top-heavy religious superstructure collapsed, I also lost my inhibitions as a writer. Above all, my fear of not keeping up with the times. In *Winter Light* I swept my house clean. Since then things have been quiet on that front.[2]

As we shall see, the statement that things were "quiet on that front" does not mean that God does not appear in some form in Bergman's films.

The film that most clearly presents the affirmation of God is *The Virgin Spring* (1960). From that film through *Fanny and Alexander* (1982) we can view the cinematic life, sickness, death and remains of God in Bergman's film work. Crucial to grasping the death of God in Bergman's corpus is the trilogy *Through a Glass Darkly, Winter Light* and *The Silence.* With these three films we have a relatively clear depiction of Bergman's move from a preoccupation with God to a preoccupation with human love, from a probing of the apparent enigma of God's existence, to an explanation and dramatization of the salvation provided by human contact and communication.

It is significant that the script for *The Virgin Spring* was not written by Bergman but by Ulla Isaksson. That Bergman, years later, was quite dissatisfied with the view of God that appears in the film is also significant. However when he first finished the film he loved it.

But when I'd finished making *The Virgin Spring* I thought I'd made one of my best films. I was delighted, shaken, I enjoyed showing it to all sorts of people . . . A fine example of how one's motifs can get all tangled up, and how limitations and weaknesses one isn't clear about— intellectual shortcomings, inability to see through one's own motives— can transform a work as it develops.[3]

In filming the story of the rape and murder of a lovely, innocent, young girl and the vengeance her father takes on her

Innocent Karin (Birgitta Pettersson) shortly before her rape and murder by goatherds (Ove Porath, Tor Isedal and Axel Duberg).

murderers, Bergman created an alternately lovely and frighteningly powerful film. When the father discovers who the murderers are, he temporarily reverts to violence and slaughters them. But having brutally taken vengeance the father repents and a miraculous spring appears at the site of the girl's death. Bergman's film is a miracle play that can still move us today. It is the film in which the loving presence of a transcendent God is most clearly affirmed. From the questioning that wound all the way through *The Seventh Seal* we have a piece of cinema that depicts God's loving forgiveness. But whatever Bergman's view of God was at the time of the making of the film, years later he rejected the view of God dramatized in the film. Discussing *The Virgin Spring* ten years after he made it Bergman said:

I wanted to make a blackly brutal mediaeval ballad in the simple form of a folk-song. But while talking it all over with the authoress, Ulla Isaksson, I began psychologizing. That was the first mistake, the introduction of a therapeutic idea: that the building of their church would heal these people. Obviously it was therapeutic; but artistically it was utterly uninteresting. And then, the introduction of a totally unanalysed idea of God. The mixture of the real active depiction of violence, which has a certain artistic potency, with all this other shady stuff—today I find it all dreadfully *triste*.[4]

I think that *The Virgin Spring* is an exceptionally good film and agree with critic Robin Wood that it has never received the attention it deserves.[5] However in terms of the cinematic depiction of God, it is a temporary pause between the struggles with faith depicted in *The Seventh Seal* and the resolution worked out in the trilogy.

After *The Seventh Seal* and prior to *The Virgin Spring,* Bergman made *Wild Strawberries* (1957) and *The Face* (1958), known in the United States as *The Magician.* The problem of God is not at the center of *Wild Strawberries*, the story of Dr. Isak Borg, moving not only to the city of Lund to receive an honorary degree, but through his memories toward an evaluation of his life. But while not at center stage, the problem of God is present. While journeying toward Lund the doctor gives a lift to three college-age youths, Viktor (Björn Bjelvenstam), an atheistic medical student, Anders (Folke Sundquist), a student for the Lutheran ministry and Sara (Bibi Andersson) whom both young men love. Humorously Bergman recounts through Sara the kind of doctrinaire argumentation in which believer and unbeliever can engage. Speaking of Viktor and Anders to Isak, Sara says:

When you left they were talking away about the existence of God. Finally they got so angry that they began shouting at each other. Then Anders grabbed Viktor's arm and tried to twist it off, and Viktor said that was a pretty lousy argument for the existence of God. Then I said that I thought they could skip God and pay some attention to me for a while instead, and then they said that I could stop babbling because I didn't understand that it was a debate of principles, and then I said that whether there was a God or not, they were real wet blankets. Then I left and they ran down the hill to settle things because each of them insisted that the other had hurt his innermost feelings. So now they're going to slug it out.[6]

Having reproved and corrected the young men for their brashness, Isak is asked by them for his judgment on the reality of God. In response, with some help from his daughter-in-law, Marianne, and Anders, the professor recites the following poem:

Where is the friend I seek everywhere?
Dawn is the time of loneliness and care.
When twilight comes I am still yearning
Though my heart is burning, burning.

Professor Isak Borg (Victor Sjöström) with his three young travelling companions, Viktor (Björn Bjelvenstam), Sara (Bibi Andersson) and Anders (Folke Sundquist).

I see His trace of glory and power,
In an ear of grain and the fragrance of a flower,
In every sign and breath of air.
His love is there.
His voice whispers in the summer breeze.[7]

This lovely poem captures both the searching for God and belief in God's omnipresence.

In *The Magician,* the mesmerist and magician Albert Emmanuel Vogler is traveling with his troupe toward Stockholm in the summer of 1846. He is hoping to have an opportunity to perform at the Royal Palace, but because they have had a shady history of performing bogus "miracles," there is a chance that they will wind up in prison. When they stay overnight at Consul Egerman's home and are more or less forced to perform before him and his guests, Bergman contrasts the magic of Vogler with the totally scientific mind of Andrew Vergerus (Gunnar Björnstrand), the royal counsellor on medicine. That Vogler's regular makeup which he wears as a disguise makes him resemble traditional depictions of Christ, plus the original title of the film, introduce again the presence of God, at least through allusion. The duel between Vergerus and Vogler focuses on a "resurrection." Prior to Vergerus' performance there has been much discussion about whether the scientific outlook exhausts the meaning of reality or whether there might be some other dimension to reality. At one point before Vogler's performance Vergerus and Vogler's wife, Manda (Ingrid Thulin), engage in the following dialogue:

VERGERUS: . . . But miracles don't happen. It's always the apparatus and the spiel which have to do the work. The clergy have the same sad experience. God is silent and people chatter.
MANDA: If just once . . .

VERGERUS: That's what they all say. If just once. For the faithless, but above all for the faithful. If just once.

MANDA: If just once—that's true.[8]

During the course of his performance Vogler seems to have died. While Vergerus is performing an autopsy on a corpse, which he mistakenly thinks is Vogler's, it seems to Vergerus that Vogler has risen from the dead. The terror that strikes the doctor momentarily casts doubt on his scientific faith. In *The Magician*, Bergman has pulled a kind of switch against contemporary established wisdom: rather than science casting doubts into the mind of the religious believer, an apparent resurrection casts doubt into the mind of the medical man who embraces scientism, the view that only science can reveal truth. In *Wild Strawberries* and *The Magician* there is no clear disbelief in God's presence. That comes in the trilogy.

The descriptive subtitles that Bergman assigned to each film in the trilogy suggest the change that happened in Bergman's vision as he created the films: *Through a Glass Darkly*—certainty achieved, *Winter Light*—certainty unmasked, *The Silence*—God's silence—the negative impression. When I discuss Bergman's view of love, I will follow his lead and approach the trilogy as primarily about human communication. But the trilogy is also about communication or lack of communication between God and us. In *Through a Glass Darkly* we receive at least two views of God; one is that of Karin, a schizophrenic who in the course of the film is losing touch with reality; the other, articulated by Karin's father, David, at the end of the film. Early in *Through a Glass Darkly* we discover that Karin is suffering from a mental disease that will become progressively worse. There is a striking scene in which Karin is alone in the house. She eerily mounts the stairs and seems to be looking to find someone. She eventually enters an empty room and has a vision of "God". She sees

God as a spider who is trying to violate her. The scene, as shot by Bergman, is extraordinarily powerful. Karin is screaming and trying to protect herself and the walls look like paper that is about to tear, suggesting the disintegration of Karin's world. Trying to explain to David, her husband Martin, and her brother Minus, Karin says:

I was frightened.
    The door opened. But the god who came out was a spider. He had six legs and moved very fast across the floor. He came up to me and I saw his face, a loathsome, evil face. And he clambered up onto me and tried to force himself into me. But I protected myself. All the time I saw his eyes. They were cold and calm. When he couldn't force himself into me, he climbed quickly up onto my breast and my face and went on up the wall. I've seen God.[9]

While the God of Karin is extremely unattractive, the God of David is appealing. When Karin is taken away to the hospital after her vision, David and Minus, both terribly shaken by Karin's breakdown, try to draw some meaning from it. David eventually confesses that he believes that God is love or perhaps that love proves God's existence and that this belief gives him hope to get through life.
    When questioned about the view of God that is expressed by Karin's hideous vision, Bergman responded,

As far as I recall, it's a question of the total dissolution of all notions of an other-worldly salvation. During those years this was going on in me all the time and being replaced by a sense of the holiness—to put it clumsily—to be found in man himself. The only holiness which really exists. A holiness wholly of this world. And I suppose that's what the final sequence tries to express. The notion of love as the only thinkable form of holiness.[10]

Karin having her vision of the spider-God in *Through a Glass Darkly*.

In *Winter Light,* pastor Tomas is struggling with the silence of God. His mistress, Marta (Ingrid Thulin), is an agnostic. In a rather dramatic scene in the midst of his struggles with faith Tomas is asked by Marta what is bothering him and he replies "God's silence."[11] An exchange between them follows and eventually Marta says:

Sometimes I think you're the limit! God's silence, God doesn't speak. God hasn't ever spoken, because he doesn't exist. It's all so unreservedly, horribly simple.[12]

This scene takes place in the vestry office of the church. Shortly after it Tomas is revisited by Jonas Persson (Max von Sydow), a fisherman in deep despair because of the threat of nuclear holocaust. Tomas was very concerned that Jonas accept his invitation to come and discuss his feelings. It is almost as though Tomas' weak faith hinges on whether he will be able to help Jonas. In his attempt to help Jonas, Tomas is brutally honest about his own vocation, about how he became a clergyman to please his parents, about how he once believed in a comfortable God that made his life secure. When he does not seem to be affecting Jonas with his confession, Tomas explains that he needs Jonas' help. He delivers a long speech that is only interrupted by Jonas' restlessness:

Well, and what if God doesn't exist? What difference does it make? Life becomes something we can understand. What a relief! And death—extinction, dissolution of body and soul. People's cruelty, their loneliness, their fear—everything becomes self-evident—transparent. Suffering is incomprehensible, so it needn't be explained. The stars out in space, worlds, heavens, all have given birth to themselves and to each other. There isn't any creator, no one who holds it all together, no immeasurable thought to make one's head spin. . . . We're alone, you

Pastor Tomas tries to grapple with the faith problem of Jonas (Max von Sydow) as Jonas' wife (Gunnel Lindblom) listens.

and I. We've betrayed the only condition under which men can live: to live together. And that's why we're so poverty-stricken, joyless and full of fear. All this stink of an antique godliness! All this supernatural helplessness, this humiliating sense of sin! You must live, Jonas. Summer's on the way. After all, the darkness won't last for ever. You've got your strawberry beds, haven't you, and your flowering jasmine? What perfume! Long hot days. It's the earthly paradise, Jonas. It's something to live for! We'll see a lot of each other, you and I. We'll become good friends, and talk to each other about this dark day. We've given gifts to each other, haven't we? You've given me your fear and I've given you a god I've killed.[13]

Tomas, overcome by his feverish chills rests his head on his hands on the table confessing that he is in a wretched state. When he looks up, Jonas has left. Tomas goes over to the window. The light through the window intensifies as Tomas says "God, my God, why have you abandoned me?"[14] The increase of light suggests Tomas' insight into the nonexistence of God. Tomas walks into the church and says "I'm free now. At last, free."[15]

The use of religious symbols as a cinematic comment on human interpersonal contact and love becomes commonplace in Bergman after *Winter Light.* Though the search for a transcendent God was real in *The Seventh Seal,* with the appearance of *Winter Light* any vertical dimension in Christianity has become horizontal, the transcendent has been reduced to the immanent.

With *The Silence* we have a world in which God is totally absent. His presence has been replaced by war tanks moving ominously through the fictional city of Timolka. Certainly by the end of the trilogy Bergman's preoccupations with God's existence and involvement in human affairs had departed. In responding to questions about the trilogy and whether after *The Silence* he had become an agnostic, which the questioner described as one who after struggling with problems just drops them, Bergman said:

> Or one might say the problem dissolves. Anyway the crux of the matter is—*the problem doesn't exist any more.* Nothing, absolutely nothing at all has emerged out of all these ideas of faith and scepticism, all these convulsions, these puffings and blowings. For many of my fellow human beings on the other hand, I'm aware that these problems still exist—and exist as a terrible reality. I hope this generation will be the last to live under the scourge of religious anxiety.[16]

Looking at the films that follow the trilogy we can find in almost every one some reference to religion or religious symbols, but the symbols point not to a transcendent God but rather to the success or failure of human love. I am convinced that Bergman as a filmmaker could not wash his consciousness of the Christian symbols that permeated his childhood, but he has put these symbols to a totally secular use. Denying a Christian interpretation that some gave to his films, and responding to an interviewer's insistence that such interpretations seem to contain a great deal of evidence, Bergman said:

> Maybe that's not so odd. I come from a world of conservative Christian thought. I've absorbed Christianity with my mother's milk. So it must be obvious that certain . . . archetypes, aren't they called—stick in one's mind, and that certain lines, certain courses of events, certain ways of behaving, become adequate symbols for what goes on in the Christian system of ideas.[17]

At the beginning of *Shame,* Jon (Max von Sydow) and Eva (Liv Ullmann) are in their cottage. It is morning and they are getting ready for the day. A church bell rings. It is not Sunday. Jon asks why it is ringing. Eva admits that she does not know.

Then a phone rings and when Eva answers, there is no one on the other end of the line. The meaningless ringing of the church bells is linked with the lack of communication suggested by the lack of response on the phone. Both are a foreshadowing of the wasteland of war that the rest of the film portrays, a wasteland in which violence is the main way of communicating. The wartorn country is the natural product of people who cannot communicate or make loving contact.

In *The Rite* artists perform something like a Mass, but its meaning is not only terrestrial rather than transcendent, it is an action that is meant to deceive as much as communicate.

In *The Passion of Anna* (1969) interpreters see much Christian symbolism.[18] Vernon Young is correct to insist that the film's title, which was originally *The Passion,* should not have been changed in the English version.[19] The new title conveys less obviously the passion motif that pervades the film.[20] The one symbol I will mention specifically is Anna's Easter Dream. In the dream Anna (Liv Ullmann) meets a group of women, one of whom sits apart from the rest. Anna is told that this woman's son is going to be executed. Anna is told that the woman is on her way to the place of execution, even though the women have tried to persuade her not to go. Anna tries to beg the woman's forgiveness but rather than a look of forgiveness Anna receives a look of scorn. The paradox of the Easter dream seems to be that there is no resurrection and forgiveness but only passion, suffering and death.[21]

In *The Touch* David (Elliot Gould), an archeologist, is doing excavation among religious ruins. He comes upon a statue of a Madonna and Child. In one scene David and Karin (Bibi Andersson), who is married to Andreas (Max von Sydow), are standing outside the church in which David discovered the Madonna and Child. David and Karin are holding hands and David comments about how close they are. Their intimacy is underscored by the ringing of the church bells. This time the bells call attention to the presence of love, albeit an illicit love. However, even that presence is precarious. Eventually David discovers that the Madonna and Child are being eaten by larvae. When David comments to Karin that the larvae are beautiful, at least as beautiful as the statue, then images of God and their reference to a more stable world no longer have much relevance.

In *Cries and Whispers* Bergman uses the symbol of the *Pietà* to convey the love between Agnes (Harriet Andersson) and Anna (Kari Sylwan). At the end of the film the only relationship that seems able to confront suffering and death is this relationship between Agnes and her maidservant, Anna. There is a shot of Anna holding Agnes in the way Mary is depicted holding Jesus in the *Pietà*. There is even a kind of resurrection in the film, in the sense that after Agnes' death, when Anna reads Agnes' diary, the truth that the deceased live on in the memories of those who loved them is pictorially illustrated.

As he did with his earlier film *Through a Glass Darkly*, Bergman takes the title of *Face to Face* from Chapter 13 of St. Paul's First Letter to the Corinthians. In that chapter Paul says that, though in this world we see God only through faith, "through a glass darkly," as it were, in heaven, after we have risen, we will see God face to face. What Bergman offers in *Face to Face* is a secular version of the resurrection. Dr. Jenny Isaksson attempts suicide. During the time when she is near death and the time in the hospital, she has four dreams. The first three dreams are about relationships in her life that have not gone well: her relationship with her grandmother, her relationship with her parents, her relationship with her patients. The fourth dream is about her own identity. In the fourth dream Jenny sees her own corpse and sets it ablaze. This burning of self suggests a death to the past and a rising to the future. Jenny rises from her suicide attempt and at the end of the film decides to continue her work.

Jenny's decision to return to work offers at least a modicum of hope for the future.

In *The Serpent's Egg* Manuela Rosenberg (Liv Ullmann), a Jewess, goes to a Catholic church, enters the sacristy and tells a priest (James Whitmore) that she has been attending Mass each morning and that she is overcome with guilt. He tells her that he and she must forgive one another. Though the scene is one of the most awkward in a Bergman film, the impression given is that the priest is more interested in a human rather than a divine forgiveness.

In *Autumn Sonata* the two people in center stage are Charlotte (Ingrid Bergman), a famous concert pianist, and her daughter, Eva (Liv Ullmann), who is married to a minister, Viktor (Holvan Bjork). Eva and Viktor have lost their three-year-old son Eric in a drowning accident. Though a minister, Viktor has no faith in God. At one point in the film he admits that whatever faith he has lives in the faith his wife has. In Eva we have a rare character in a Bergman film, at least since *The Virgin Spring*. Eva believes that her three-year-old son lives beyond the grave and she feels very close to him. She says,

He's living another life, but at any moment we can reach each other, there's no dividing line, no insurmountable wall. Sometimes, of course, I wonder what it looks like—the reality where my little boy is living and breathing. At the same time I know it can't be described, as it's a world of liberated feelings. It's much harder for Viktor than it is for me. He says he can't believe in God any more because God lets children die— be burned alive or shot or starved or go mad. I try to explain to him that there's no difference between children and grown-ups, since the grown-ups are still children who have to live disguised as grown-ups. To me, man is a tremendous creation, an inconceivable thought; and in man there is everything, from the highest to the lowest, just as in life; and man is God's image; and in God there is everything, vast forces, and then the devils are created and the saints and the prophets and the obscurantists and the artists and the iconoclasts. Everything exists side by side, one thing penetrating the other. It's like huge patterns changing all the time, do you know what I mean? In that way there must also be countless realities, not only the reality we perceive with our blunt senses, but a tumult of realities arching above and around each other, inside and outside. It's merely fear and priggishness to believe in any limits. *There are no limits.* Neither to thoughts nor to feelings. It's anxiety that sets the limits, don't you think so too? When you play the slow movement of Beethoven's *Hammerklavier Sonata,* you must surely feel you're moving in a world without limitations, inside an immense motion that you can never see through or explore. It's the same with Jesus. He burst asunder the laws and the limitations with an entirely new feeling that no one had heard of before—love. No wonder people were afraid and angry, just as they nearly always try to sneak off in alarm when some big emotion overwhelms them, though they eat their hearts out pining for their withered and deadened feelings.[22]

Even in her protestation of faith Eva anticipates Charlotte's judgment that Eva's faith is neurotic. My own judgment is that with Eva, who definitely has problems relating, Bergman is presenting a believer who finds enormous consolation in her faith. Though there is no evidence from his films or interviews that Bergman experiences that consolation, he is presenting in Eva a faith that obviously helps people.

Bergman's personal, emotional reaction to his experience of religion seems to be articulated in the film that many see as the culmination of his cinematic career. In *Fanny and Alexander* the stern, sterile bishop (Jan Malmsjö) is the typical representative of institutional religion in a Bergman film. There does not seem to be a trace of human warmth in him. He is contrasted with the warm loving Isak (Erland Josephson), who eventually, through magic, rescues Alexander from the clutches of the bishop. However Alexander (Gertil Guve), who is some kind of stand-in for young Ingmar,[23] articulates a view of God which sums up Bergman's emotional reaction to his perception of his stern religious upbringing. Much of *Fanny and Alexander* recalls what Steene has identified as the sensuous and magic world associated with the apartment of Bergman's grandmother. But the other stern and moralistic world is also present, and the God who represents that world is rejected by Alexander. Having escaped from the bishop's house through the magic of Isak, Alexander has three strange experiences during the night while staying at Isak's house. It is difficult to tell whether these events are hallucinations or dreams or what. They are most important for their thematic material. In each, Alexander's rejection of God is evident. In the first experience Alexander has a vision of his deceased father, Oscar (Allan Edwall). Alexander expresses his anger at his father and says:

You say you feel sorry for us. That's just talk, Papa. Why can't you go to God and tell him to kill the bishop. That is his department. Or is it so that God doesn't give a damn about you? About any of us? Have you even *seen* God over there on the other side? I bet you haven't even found out what chance there is of getting close to God. You've just drifted around as usual, worrying about us children and Mama.[24]

In the second experience Alexander has an encounter with Isak's twenty-year-old son, Aron (Mats Bergman), who is a magician. Using puppets in a dark room Aron frightens Alexander and the following conversation takes place:

ALEXANDER: This is the end of me. Isn't it? Who's behind the door?
VOICE: It is God behind the door.
ALEXANDER: Can't you come out?

Alexander (Bertil Guve) and Fanny (Pernilla Allwin) on the edges of the adult world.

VOICE: No one living may see God's face.

ALEXANDER: What do you want with me?

VOICE: I only want to prove that I exist.

ALEXANDER: I am very grateful. Thank you.

VOICE: For me you are merely an insignificant little grain of dust. Did you know that?

ALEXANDER: No.

VOICE: Besides, you are unkind to your sisters and your parents, you are insolent to your teachers, and you think nasty thoughts. I don't really know why I let you live, Alexander.

ALEXANDER: No.

VOICE: *Holiness!* Alexander!

ALEXANDER: What?

VOICE: Holiness! The cow that tossed the dog, that worried the cat, that killed the rat, and so on. Do you understand what I mean?

ALEXANDER: I don't think I do.

VOICE: God is the world and the world is God. That's all there is to it.

ALEXANDER: Please forgive me, but if it's as you say, then I am God too.

VOICE: You are not God at all, you are just a stuck-up little brat.

ALEXANDER: I can't see that I'm any more stuck-up than God is. I'd be grateful if God would prove the opposite.

VOICE: *Love,* Alexander!

ALEXANDER: What love?

VOICE: I am speaking of *My* love. God's love. God's love for Man. (Pause) Well?

ALEXANDER: Oh yes, I've heard of that love.

VOICE: Is there anything greater than love?

ALEXANDER: Well, if there is it would be His Grace the bishop's cockstand. I can't think of anything else as I'm only ten years old and haven't much experience.

VOICE: That was the right answer but a pretty cheeky one. Would you like me to perform a miracle?

ALEXANDER: What can you do?

VOICE: I am almighty. Have you forgotten?

ALEXANDER: I haven't forgotten but I don't believe it, because you're always harping on being almighty. If you really were almighty it would be so obvious that neither you nor the bishop would have to prove your omnipotence every Sunday.[25]

After Aron reveals his identity he asks Alexander what he thinks about God. To Alexander's statement that if there is a God "then he's a shit and piss God and I'd like to kick him in the arse," Aron replies:

I think your theory is very interesting, my dear Alexander. Moreover, it appears to be fairly well justified. I for my part am an atheist. If one has been brought up as a magician and has learnt all the tricks in child-hood, then one can do without supernatural interference! A sorcerer like me prefers to show what is understandable; it is up to the specta-tors to provide what is not.[26]

The third encounter is with Ismael (Stina Ekblad), Isak's other son who is disturbed and kept behind locked doors. In this encounter Ismael seems to be able to read Alexander's mind and he gives Alexander a vision of the bishop burning to death, which actually happens. At one point Ismael says, "The truth about the world is the truth about God."[27]

The three encounters dramatize the irrelevance of any belief in God as One who cares for human beings. Aron has opted for art over religion, Ismael seems to have transcended the God-question. Both dissenters are alter egos for Alexander. Indeed, Aron's control as an artist and his overcoming of fear through art is reminiscent of Bergman's claims of overcoming the terror of death and his religious anxieties through the creation of films.[28] When Ismael, prior to reading Alexander's mind about the bish-op's death, told Alexander to write his name, the boy wrote not his own name but "Ismael." It is as though Alexander is meeting the frightening, wild part of himself. This is emphasized by the following interchange:

ISMAEL: Perhaps we are the same person. Perhaps we have no limits; perhaps we flow into each other, stream through each other, boundlessly and magnificently. You bear terrible thoughts; it is almost painful to be near you. At the same time it is enticing. Do you know why?

ALEXANDER: I don't think I want to know.

ISMAEL: Evil thoughts have a considerable enticement. Most people cannot materialize it and that is perhaps fortunate for mankind. Anyway, it's all primitive and barbarous! For example, you make an image of someone you dislike and stick pins in it. It's rather a clumsy method when you think of the swift and straight ways that evil thoughts can go.

ALEXANDER: I don't think I want to talk to you about this.

ISMAEL: You're a strange little person, Alexander. You don't want to talk about what you are thinking of every moment.

ALEXANDER: If that's so—Yes, it's true.[29]

I think that Frank Gado is correct: in Ismael, Alexander and Bergman face the wildness that empowers the imagination.[30] Through Alexander and the child's (and Bergman's) alter egos Aron and Ismael, Bergman has dramatized his escape from a preoccupation with God's existence, an escape that has gone in one direction since the trilogy. From *The Seventh Seal* to *Fanny and Alexander* Bergman's cinematic God has been transformed into a symbol used to highlight what is significant in human interpersonal relations.

4

Death:
The Inevitable Journey

THE SEARCH FOR meaning that is incarnated in a Bergman film almost always takes place against a background stained by the reality of death. Our discussion of *The Seventh Seal* suggested how central to Bergman's consciousness the reality of death is. Like existentialist philosophers such as Heidegger, Sartre and Camus, Bergman sees that the reality of death puts a question mark on all human activities.[1] Existentialist philosopher Nikolai Berdyaev wrote:

Death is the most profound and significant fact of life, raising the least of mortals above the mean commonplaces of life. The fact of death alone gives true depth to the question as to the meaning of life. Life in this world has meaning just because there is death; if there were no death in our world, life would be meaningless. The meaning is bound up with the end. If there were no end, i.e., if life in our world continued for ever, there would be no meaning in it.[2]

In Bergman's films people are trying either to comprehend death or to live meaningfully in the face of death. Bergman has confessed "All my so-called artistic expression is only a desperate protest against death. Despite this, I keep on . . ."[3] Death can seem to reduce all human activities to the absurd.[4] In the face of death what can a person do? What if any human activities are of any significance or importance? If death throws a question mark over all human activities is there any one thing that allows man to positively respond to death? Is life "sound and fury signifying nothing"? Or is it a journey that has some value? What is Bergman's view of death and what response does he offer to the reality of death?

In the body of films we are considering two of the earliest examples of Bergman's preoccupation with death are *The Seventh Seal* and *Wild Strawberries*. It is against the ogre of death that the knight and the doctor conduct their search for meaning. For each time is running out and they fear that their lives have been wasted, counterfeit preoccupations with projects that are ultimately meaningless. Each is grasping for some liberating insight as death approaches. In *Wild Strawberries* there is an aerial shot of the car in which Dr. Isak Borg is traveling to Lund to receive his honorary degree. The shot makes the limousine look like a hearse driving along a winding road. Once again the shot is quintessential Bergman and visually expresses the question at the heart of the film: what meaning does Dr. Isak Borg's life have in the face of his death?

Bergman has recounted how *Wild Strawberries* was born. As a child he spent a great deal of time with his grandmother who lived during the winters in a big old-fashioned flat in Uppsala. In the autumn of 1956 Bergman had to drive to Uppsala. His grandmother had lived at Nedre Slottsgatan 14. Bergman confessed:

That's where I lived as a little boy, and that sort of world had made a strong impression upon me.

That morning in the car I felt a sudden impulse to drive up to Slottsgatan 14. It was autumn, and a faint sun had begun to fall on the cathedral and the clock was just striking five. I went into the little cobblestone yard. Then I went up into the house and took hold of the door knob to the kitchen door, which still had its coloured glass pattern; and a feeling ran quickly through me: suppose I open it? Supposing old Lalla (our old cook, she was) is standing inside there, in her big apron, making porridge for breakfast, as she did so many times when I was little? Suppose I could suddenly walk into my childhood?

Nowadays I don't suffer much from nostalgia, but I used to. I think Maria Wine (Swedish poetess) has said somewhere that one sleeps in one's childhood's shoe. Well that's exactly how it was. Then it struck me: supposing I make a film of someone coming along, perfectly realistically, and suddenly opening a door and walking into his childhood? And then opening another door and walking out into reality again? And then walking round the corner of the street and coming into some other period of his life, and everything still alive and going on as before? That was the real starting point of *Wild Strawberries*.[5]

In the spring of 1957 Bergman began to write the script about a doctor who had, Bergman said, "cut off everything around him—as I'd done."[6] Even though he had used his own experience Bergman claims that it was not until he had been at the script a while before he realized that he had given the doctor his own initials. Bergman said he had consciously chosen the name Isak because he thought of the old doctor as icy.[7] One interviewer told Bergman that the very strained relationship between the doctor and his son, Ewald, he saw as a criticism of the traditional structure of the family, centered on a patriarchal father-figure. Bergman's response is another piece of evidence indicating how similar the director feels to his creature:

Obviously. But all this business about Ewald and his father is so tremendously personal, I can't sort it out. Nor can I sort out the relationship between Isak Borg and his mother.[8]

Concerning Isak's relationship to his mother and to his son, Ewald, Robin Wood points out that the coldness in the Borg family passes from generation to generation.

The "theme" of *Wild Strawberries*, incarnated in the successive generations of Borgs, is death-in-life, emotional-spiritual atrophy. It is not simply repeated from generation to generation but developed. We see it in Isak's much admired, aged mother (Naima Wifstrand) a hard, mean-minded complacency masquerading as a disillusioned realism of outlook: her children only visit her when they want to borrow money (doubtless true enough!); the relics of the past, photographs of her sons as children, etc., have become mere "rubbish." She clutches her souvenirs because they are about all she has left, but they have long since ceased to have any meaning for her. Her life is all peevish, self-pitying bitterness: she cannot see herself as she is; her existence is a kind of spiritual prison.[9]

Isak has a chance of coming back to life because his daughter-in-law has honestly told him what a cold mean person he has been. Wood points out that Ewald has the best chance of growth precisely because he is the most wretched and tormented.[10] The pain is an opportunity for growth for Ewald because it indicates some insight into his death-in-life existence while his grandmother has none.

Crucial to seeing that the death-in-life theme is at the center of *Wild Strawberries* is the nightmare that Borg has at the beginning of his day's adventure. The filming of the dream, which Bergman says in its basic ingredients is one he has had often,[11] was exceptionally well-done. In the dream Borg is walking along the street on which he usually takes his morning constitutional. However, the street is now deserted. That the street is deserted contributes to the strange milieu. The sun seems to give no warmth. The large clock has a blank dial and Borg's pocket watch is also without hands. The large eyeglasses suspended from the street clock have been smashed. Borg sees a man who wears a soft felt hat as Borg does but when the man turns around Borg sees that the man has no face. When Borg puts his watch to his ear he hears his own heart beating. As a bell tolls a hearse moves toward the petrified doctor. The hearse loses a wheel that almost hits Isak and bumps into a lamppost. The coffin falls out of the hearse and when Isak looks into the coffin he discovers the corpse is himself dressed in the frock coat he is to wear at the ceremony at Lund.

After his succinct description of this dream Frank Gado comments:

Besides introducing death as the keynote to the day, the dream, . . . functions as a prologue. Virtually every one of its strange occurrences has a parallel in the events to follow but the most important of them is the eerie creaking of springs, like an infant's wail, as the hearse ejects the coffin. This image of spiritual stillbirth strikes to the film's thematic core. Isak, whose dreams tell him that all his life has been "dead although alive," has fostered a replica of himself in his son, and at the old man's side during the trip sits his daughter-in-law Marianne, pregnant with the heir of these lifeless generations.[12]

The key points of the dream are that Borg's time is running out and that he should confront his emotional and spiritual death before he experiences his physical death.

Two of Bergman's later films, *Cries and Whispers* and *Face to Face*, the former a masterpiece and the latter merely brilliant, are clearly structured around the problem of death. Both films are dramatic, highly detailed cinematic depictions of people struggling to live meaningfully. The presence of death in each film intensifies the struggle.

In *Cries and Whispers* Bergman situates four women (three

sisters and a maid who has long been with the family) in a large manor house, all the rooms of which are painted in red. The reason they are painted in red is connected with what Bergman is trying to do in the film. In a letter he wrote to his co-workers as they were about to begin making *Cries and Whispers* Bergman wrote:

... it is important that our decor never be obvious. It should be flexible, enclosing, elusive, and present, evocative without being obtrusive. There is a peculiarity about it, however: all our interiors are red, of various shades. Don't ask me why it must be so, because I don't know. I have puzzled over this myself, and each explanation has seemed more comical than the last. The bluntest but also the most valid is probably that the whole thing is something internal and that ever since my childhood I have pictured the inside of the soul as a moist membrane in shades of red.[13]

Bergman's inability to clearly explain why the walls are red fits in with his and Maritain's description of how a work of art is conceived[14] but Bergman's depiction of the inside of the soul as red relates to the theme of *Cries and Whispers*. What he is trying to do in *Cries and Whispers* is film the human soul searching for love.[15] The search is precarious, even treacherous, because of the reality of death. I don't think it is an overstatement to say that the film presents a metaphysics of death. Writing in *The New York Times* about first-class films such as *Sunday, Bloody Sunday* and *The Last Picture Show* and comparing *Cries and Whispers* to them, Ronald Friedland wrote of Bergman's film:

When we see it, we know we are in another dimension, the dimension of myth. Bergman knows that the specific society makes no difference. Money, furniture, servants, life in the woods, on the farm, in a Marxist utopia, cannot solve the loneliness and doubt fostered by death. Psychology cannot help here.[16]

As he was also to do in *Face to Face,* Bergman opts in *Cries and Whispers* for a more radical examination of death than psychology can provide. Bergman is searching for the ultimate meaning of death, and therefore rather than appeal to psychology he makes a movie that is a mixture of myth and metaphysics.

Each of the four women in *Cries and Whispers* is threatened by death: one by physical death, the other three by emotional death. Agnes is dying of cancer. Her maidservant Anna has been caring for her and now that she is in the last stages, her two sisters Maria (Liv Ullmann) and Karin (Ingrid Thulin) have come to stay with her. The film explores the relationship between the four women and it does so in brilliant visual images. Though Bergman authors his own screenplays, and though many of them make exceptionally good reading, it is impossible to categorize Bergman as a writer rather than a filmmaker. His films are strongly visual and *Cries and Whispers* may be the most visually beautiful of all.[17] Perhaps more than any other director in the history of filmmaking, Bergman fulfills critic Andre Bazin's description of a director as someone who writes in film.[18]

Agnes seems resigned to her death. She doesn't complain about the pain and seems to be trying to face her death with a kind of courage. Of the three sisters, she seems far and away the least selfish and self-centered. Her elder sister by two years, Karin, is trapped in an unhappy marriage. She is cold and seems to be disillusioned with life. Though she desires love and affection her desires have been unfulfilled and she now seems closed in on herself. The youngest of the three, Maria, is like a spoiled child. She is playful, a flirt and seems thoroughly superficial and self-centered. Anna is shy and taciturn but strong. A deep affection has grown up between Anna and Agnes, probably due in part to the fact that Agnes took care of Anna and her little daughter until the child died at the age of three. However the relationship between the two women has endured beyond the child's death. The personalities of the women are given to us not merely through ordinary action and dialogue but through flashbacks, surrealistic scenes and through events that, though they are rooted in fact, have more the reality of a dream than an actual happening. Bergman's depiction of the plot and characters is far from linear and realistic, and this is why Bergman seemed to hesitate to even call *Cries and Whispers* a film. In his letter to his co-workers he referred to *Cries and Whispers* as "the film (or whatever we're going to call our project)."[19]

Both Karin and Maria seem emotionally and spiritually dead. In a series of surrealistic dream-like scenes Bergman reveals the personalities of the two sisters. I call the scenes dreamlike for want of a better term. Though the scenes are quite meaningful, providing us with insights into the characters and adding enormously to the development of the film, the events that are depicted are not spatio-temporal events that actually happen. They are more like visual interpretations of the character's souls.[20]

One of the scenes shows the superficial, self-centered Maria with her husband who has just knifed himself. He is dying and pleading for help. She looks on with a kind of fascination as he is dying. That he appears perfectly healthy at the end of the film makes clear the nature of the earlier scene. Two other scenes underline the frigidity of Karin and her inability to either give or receive love. Karin has come to believe that life is nothing but a tissue of lies. In one surrealistic scene, the one scene in Bergman's work which I would say clearly violates canons of taste, as she and her husband are preparing for bed, she cuts her vagina with a piece of glass and spreads the blood on her face in order to disgust her husband.

In another surrealistic scene, this one quite powerful visually, Maria reaches out to Karin for affection. Bergman shows the lovely faces of the two women in closeup. Maria says:

I want us to be friends. I want us to touch each other, I want us to talk to each other. After all, we're sisters. We have so many memories in common—we can talk about our childhood! Karin, my dear, it's so strange that we don't touch one another, that we only talk impersonally. Why won't you be my friend? . . .[21]

As Maria tries to touch Karin, the latter says "No, don't touch me . . . Don't touch me. I hate any sort of contact. Don't come near me."[22]

Eventually, Maria and Karin, as though out of a mutual impulse and in a burst of affection, embrace. Later, at the end of the film, Karin denies that this ever happened. Though all these scenes are filmed to suggest that they are not ordinary spatiotemporal events they reveal the personalities of the two sisters. With their sister's death imminent, they struggle to be affectionate and loving. Maria wants to overcome her shallowness and her deceit, and Karin wants to be warm and affectionate. Each sees that something is terribly wrong with her life. In the film only Anna and Agnes seem to be able to relate in a loving way. Bergman's view of death, his belief that loving people is the only possible response to the horror of death, is clearly depicted in two dreamlike scenes near the end of the film. The two scenes provide a kind of resurrection motif to the end of the film. One scene is a dream-like sequence, the other, the final scene in the film, is a flashback.

The dreamlike sequence occurs after Agnes' death. From the room where Agnes' corpse is laid out whispers are heard. Able to speak, Agnes' corpse calls out to the three women. When they hear Agnes and see her stretching her arms out to them, Karin and Maria, screaming, flee the room. They do not love Agnes enough to go to her. They are frightened by her death. Only Anna responds in love. She remains in the room and embraces Agnes. In some way the love between the two women has conquered death. Even death cannot destroy love.

The second scene underlines that Agnes' life was meaningful in spite of the suffering she underwent. After Agnes' funeral Anna is reading Agnes' diary. As she reads we hear Agnes' voice on the soundtrack reciting the words of the diary and we have a flashback of a lovely sunny afternoon in which the four women were together. All of them are in white dresses. As we view this beautiful scene we hear Agnes' voice speaking the words from her diary:

The people I'm most fond of in the world were with me. I could hear them chatting round about me, I felt the presence of their bodies, the warmth of their hands. I closed my eyes tightly, trying to cling to the moment and thinking, come what may, this is happiness. I can't wish for anything better. Now, for a few minutes, I can experience perfection. And I feel a great gratitude to my life, which gives me so much.[23]

Then Bergman has the screen go totally red except for an inscription in white which reads "And so the cries and whispers fade away." Agnes is dead. Karin and Maria are emotionally dead in the sense that one is closed to all relationships and the other is incapable of any deep relationships. The film is a powerful, highly visual exploration of the experience of death in various forms.

Face to Face is also an exploration of death.[24] It may be Bergman's most personal work. Probably in her role as Jenny in the film, Liv Ullmann is articulating Bergman's feelings when she speaks about death:

As a child I was afraid of death. It seemed to be all around me. I've followed the principle that now I'll make up my mind to feel like this and I feel like this. I decided I'd never be afraid of death and the dead. I decided to ignore the fact that people died every day, every moment. Death didn't exist any more except as a vague idea, and that was that.[25]

Face to Face dramatizes a confrontation with death. While she is substituting for another doctor at a psychiatric clinic, psychiatrist Jenny Isaakson is summering at her grandparents' home, the home in which she was brought up. Jenny's husband and daughter are away for the summer. During this visit Jenny's past catches up with her and she undergoes a severe psychological crisis.

Jenny's problems are suggested in one of the early scenes. She is trying to get a patient, Maria (Kari Sylwan), to respond. Maria seems to be in an autistic half-trance. As Jenny is trying to get Maria to respond the autistic woman says "Poor Jenny." The suggestion is that Jenny is worse off than Maria. The latter is psychologically sick, Jenny is spiritually sick. After this scene Jenny is discussing the case with another psychiatrist, a cynical man who remarks that mental illnesses are the worst scourge on earth and that the next worse is the curing of them.

Throughout *Face to Face*, Bergman plays two images against each other. The one is a lovely stained glass window depicting a flower. The window is in the apartment of Jenny's grandparents. The other image is an old woman dressed in black who appears to Jenny from time to time during the film. One of the woman's eyes is quite enlarged. The picture of the flower symbolizes life, the old woman symbolizes death. Like the character Death in *The Seventh Seal*, the presence of the old woman is telling Jenny that her time is running out. The loud ticking of clocks that often accompanies the woman's appearance emphasizes this, as on one occasion the cessation of ticking emphasizes that Jenny's

Emotionally ill Maria (Kari Sylwan) confronts her spiritually ill psychiatrist, Dr. Jenny Isaakson (Liv Ullmann).

time is almost gone. When the tensions and struggles that plague Jenny become too much for her Jenny attempts suicide by taking an overdose of pills. She is saved by a friend, Dr. Tomas Jacobs (Erland Josephson), who finds her near death in her grandparents' apartment. As Jenny hovers near death she has four dreams. Once again these dreams are more than dreams. In each of them she confronts death and also some significant aspect of her own life. In each dream Jenny is wearing a long red dress. If we recall Bergman's impression of the soul as a red moist membrane then the dress probably suggests Jenny's soul. Certainly the confrontation in each dream touches upon a crucial relationship in Jenny's life, a relationship which she ought to work out if she is going to survive and live a relatively healthy life.

The first dream focuses on her relationship with her grandparents and her view of death, the second on her work, the third on her relationship with her parents and the fourth with her psychologically ill and spiritually dead self. In each dream Bergman gives us insights into what has moved Jenny to attempt suicide. Her grandmother was a domineering woman; her work is meaningless and unfulfilling to her; the insensitivity of her parents has given her deep feelings of guilt and of being unloved. The final dream in which Jenny observes herself in a coffin and then sets the coffin on fire suggests symbolically that Jenny has somehow transcended her past.

After the dreams Jenny delivers a long speech that ties together a number of the insights about herself that have been revealed in the dreams. Liv Ullmann is nothing short of brilliant in her delivery of this speech. At the beginning she says:

We act the play. We learn our lines. We know what people want us to say. We lie. In the end it is not even deliberate . . .[26]

Dr. Jenny Isaakson tearfully reenacts her relationship with her grandmother.

In part of the speech Jenny carries on an imaginary dialogue between herself and her grandmother.

You can't wear that dress today. It's your Sunday best. You'll never manage that, my dear. Let me help you. Using lipstick, are you? . . . I'll do as I like. You're not going to order me around. You're a goddamn stupid bitch. I hate you and I could kill you . . . If you lock me in the closet I'll die. I'll be good if only you don't lock me in the closet. Please, please Grandma, forgive me for everything, but I can't live if I have to be locked in the closet. . . .[27]

The film's theme of Jenny trying to confront herself and others "face to face" is set against the background of death. The periodic appearance of the old woman highlights the point that if Jenny is going to make any sense of her life she is going to have to do it in the face of death. It is the presence of death that forces Jenny to confront her life.

After she leaves the hospital Jenny returns to her grandparents' home. She stands in the doorway to their bedroom and watches her grandmother try to comfort her grandfather who is becoming senile. She is touched by their love for one another. On the soundtrack we hear Jenny say, "For a moment I knew that love embraces everything, even death." Then Jenny calls the hospital to announce that she will be at work the next morning. Bergman cuts to the stained glass window. After a beam of sunlight shines through it Bergman dissolves the shot and his film ends.

While *Cries and Whispers* and *Face to Face* raise their questions about the meaning of life and death in relation to one character's death, *Shame* raises its questions in relation to the kind of mass death that accompanies war. When *Shame* appeared some critics thought that Bergman had left behind the themes that previously preoccupied him and made a clear thematically uncomplicated war film.[28] If *Shame* was nothing but an anti-war film it would still be powerful. Yet it is more than that. It raises Bergman's questions about "Life, Love and Death" but it raises them in terms of the violence of war. *Shame* treats death on several levels: physical death, the death of love, emotional death, artistic death and the death of a culture and a society.

Jan (Max von Sydow) and Eva (Liv Ullmann) are two violinists. They played in a symphony orchestra until it was disbanded because of the civil war that is spreading through the country. Though childless they seem to be happily married. Early in the film Eva seems the stronger of the two and has to console and comfort Jan when he has doubts about himself. By having Jan and Eva as members of a symphony orchestra Bergman admits that he was contrasting the world of art with the chaotic world of violence and war.

The main thing, as I saw it, was that an orchestra is an orderly, a disciplined world, a trifle authoritative, and with very strict working patterns. What I wanted to show most, I suppose, was that as long as Jan enjoyed such conditions, he hung together well. So does his wife, afterwards, too. The only connection with their personalities as artists is his fine 18th century instrument, which has gone through the Napoleonic wars and survived all sorts of adventures, but which gets smashed to pieces. In some way the man is part and parcel of his instrument— the instant his instrument is smashed, his entire view of life crumbles, too. He is transformed.[29]

Early in the film there are intimations that the civil war will become worse. Though Jan and Eva try to stay distant from the war they eventually are drawn into it. When they are, their lives become threatened. The destruction of the instrument to which Bergman refers suggests numerous endings: the end of their previous way of living for Jan and Eva, the ending of Jan's former personality, the ending of art and civilization in the face of war. In the film, death stains all human activities. It is significant that the film is a fable about war. By not identifying the country in which the civil war is happening Bergman makes the threat of violence and death especially ominous.

Early in the film, while the couple is still trying to stay aloof from the war, Bergman does a number of things to contrast the stability that the couple is trying to retain in their lives with the impending doom that war brings. Though the couple wants to be non-political there is no escape, no exit from the human community and its suffering, even its self-inflicted suffering. There is a scene in an antique shop that highlights the death of the couple's desired style of living. Robin Wood's comment on this scene is insightful.

The scene in the antique shop, the characters surrounded by various emblems of civilization, is very beautiful, the attitude complex but defined with great exactness. Bergman's humanity is nowhere clearer than in his presentation of the antique dealer. We see him as a man insulated from reality, politically ignorant and uncommitted, shut up amid relics of the past, hoping to convince the military authorities that his weak foot is bad enough to insure him a safe office job, or perhaps get him discharged. Yet we cannot but view him with sympathy and a certain respect: he is a civilized and gentle human being. Then there is the Meissen musical ornament, useless, artificial, unjustifiable in a world where people starve to death, are tortured, persecuted, massacred, yet by virtue of its very uselessness embodying the concept of civilization in its purest form. Amid these (the other objects) the three characters sip wine together, the sense of civilized communion balanced by the sense of valediction, the antique dealer's intuition that not only his life but his way of life is nearing its end.[30]

Just prior to the scene in the antique shop, Jan and Eva have met Major Jacobi (Gunnar Björnstrand) on the ferry to the mainland. The meeting between the couple and the Major is quite cordial. Later however, as the civil war worsens, Jacobi submits the two of them to a frightening interrogation. Jan and Eva don't know of what they are guilty, if anything. After they are released the specter of violence, war and death becomes stronger. Eventually Jan and Eva are totally involved, so involved that Jan's personality changes drastically. He becomes a killer. He is responsible for Jacobi's assassination and he coldbloodedly kills a teenage soldier who can't defend himself. In this and other scenes, Bergman depicts the horror and senselessness of the civil war. It's like Camus' plague: it touches everyone yet its origin and purpose are not clear.

The similarity between Bergman's vision as depicted in *Shame* and that of the French existentialist atheist has been pointed out by others. *Shame* certainly bears a similarity to Camus's *The Fall* in that both "works deal with the theme of personal and societal guilt and man's responsibility for the absurd state of destructive conflict in which he finds himself."[31] However, there are more striking evidences in the film of Jean-Paul Sartre's philosophy. Without claiming that Bergman was consciously influenced by Sartre, I am struck by the Sartreian themes in the film. The Sartreian view of love is clearly present in Bergman's film. In *Being and Nothingness* Sartre argues that two persons, or to use terminology closer to that of Sartre, two conscious freedoms can never successfully love one another.[32] Two freedoms as they try to relate in love are condemned to either masochism or sadism. If any relationship is to endure, then one must submit to the other and become a possession of that other. One must cease to be free. The one who surrenders freedom is a masochist; the one who possesses, who lives off the

Eva (Liv Ullmann) confronts the horror and senselessness of war in *Shame*.

surrender of the other, is a sadist. A successful love relationship is impossible.

The love between Jan and Eva, which Jan confesses so touchingly early in the film, is eventually reduced to a sado-masochistic relationship. When Jan's personality changes through the violence of war he treats Eva like a thing he possesses.

One of the most powerful images to convey the horror of death takes place at the end of *Shame*. Jan and Eva are in a lifeboat with some other survivors of the war. The boat is adrift amidst a sea of dead bodies. There are hundreds of dead soldiers floating around and the boat drifts slowly through them. As Jan is dozing off, totally unmoved by the presence of the bodies, he stares at the sailor-captain of the boat. As though he cannot bear the stare of Jan—one thinks of Sartre's famous line "Hell is other people" in *No Exit*—the sailor-captain slips over the side of the boat. With no reaction at all Jan returns to sleep. This closing image of the boat adrift amidst the dead bodies is powerful and horrible. It is a perfect image for the meaninglessness and absurdity that death can convey. However it is not Bergman's ultimate response to death. Critic Pauline Kael, in calling *Shame* a flawless work and a masterly vision, was correct in her succinct description of the film: "Treating the most dreaded of all subjects, the film makes one feel elated. The subject is our responses to death, but a work of art is a true sign of life."[33]

Shame is about our responses to death. But the film does not contain Bergman's final word on death. For that word, Bergman's vision of art and love must be considered.

5

Art: Hope
with Grey Hairs

IN ALMOST EVERY Bergman film one of the central characters is an artist. In *The Magician* there is Albert Vogler; in *Through a Glass Darkly* the father is a novelist; in *Persona* there is an actress Elizabeth Vogler; in *Hour of the Wolf* (1968) Johan is a painter; in *Shame* Jan and Eva are musicians; in *The Rite* those under suspicion are actors; in *The Serpent's Egg* Manuela is a singer; in *Autumn Sonata* Charlotte is a concert pianist; in *Fanny and Alexander* a whole family has roots in the theater. The frequent appearance of an artist at center stage in Bergman's films causes us to suspect that his preoccupations include the role of the artist and the function of art. Since his films are so personal, and in a way autobiographical, the appearance of artists is almost to be expected. Yet we must avoid a too-easy identification of the artist in the film with the artist making the film. A *caveat* for us would be a response that Bergman made to a critic John Simon. The critic suggested to the director that at least in some of his films, the Bergman figure is Max von Sydow. Bergman responded:

No, no, not at all, I say, like Flaubert, "Madame Bovary, c'est moi." I am all of them, I am inside all of them. It's not especially Max von Sydow or Gunnar Björnstrand or Ingrid Thulin.[1]

103

There is something of Bergman in all his characters. The appearance in film after film of artists allows us to see a vision of art and the artist that Bergman holds. Of course the masterpiece *Persona* in a really unique way has a strongly autobiographical element to it. But in spite of the strongly personal and autobiographical dimension of his work, it would be a mistake to think that Bergman is merely involved in self-reflection through the medium of film. Bergman's reflections on the artist should be kept within his broader vision of the role of art and indeed his vision of the meaning of personal existence.[2] Noting again that Bergman is not composing philosophical tracts, I nevertheless do agree with Paisley Livingstone that Bergman is after understanding.[3] Some have claimed that Bergman is Albert Emmanuel Vogler in *The Magician*, out to fascinate and frighten audiences with his magic lantern. However, when asked which of the characters in that film he most admired, Bergman said it was Vergerus the scientist because "I like his dream of finding out the truth about magic."[4] Bergman wants to understand, and what he especially wants to understand is the meaning and magic of art.[5]

Another element in Bergman's films that underlines the director's preoccupation with art and the artist are the frequent appearance in the films of a film, a play or theatrical performance of some kind. In *The Magician* Vogler is pressured to perform; in *Through a Glass Darkly* Karin and Minus act out a play for their father; in *The Silence* copulation takes place in a movie house while a film is being projected; in *Persona* we have a glimpse, not only of Elizabeth Vogler's performance as Electra, but also of Bergman and cameraman Sven Nykvist filming that performance; in *Hour of the Wolf* there is a puppet show; in *The Rite* there is a performance by the acting troupe; in *The Touch* we see a slide show of photographs of a family; in *Face to Face* there is a concert; in *The Serpent's Egg* there is a performance in a

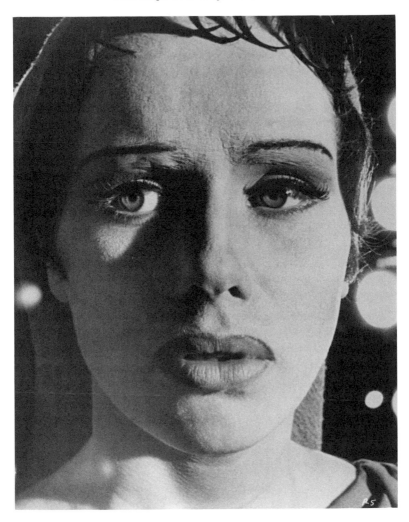

Elizabeth (Liv Ullmann) mute in her role as Electra in *Persona*. The lights of a movie camera, Bergman's reminder to us that we are watching a film, can be seen at the right.

dance hall; in *Autumn Sonata* Charlotte and Eva play the piano for each other; and in *Fanny and Alexander* there are moments from a stage production.

It is helpful to put Bergman's view of art into the broad perspective of his view of human life. Probably the most famous statement of Bergman on art is what has come to be known as "the snakeskin speech." In 1965 Bergman received the Erasmus prize in Amsterdam. He wrote the snakeskin speech as his acceptance speech at the presentation. On the surface, Bergman seems incredibly pessimistic, but a more careful reading reveals an honesty and a vision of his own work that I think is both accurate and profound. Unfortunately the speech contains several comments that, if quoted out of context, would badly distort its meaning when considered in its entirety.

Bergman began the talk[6] noting that in his case artistic creativity always manifested itself as a kind of hunger. Though as a child he wanted to attract the attention of others to whatever he was doing, e.g., progress in drawing, Bergman confesses that because he never excited enough interest in his fellow human beings he eventually became a daydreamer. But the desire to share his dreams would never disappear, and so he became a movie-maker because cinema gave him the possibility of communicating with the world around him "in a language that is literally spoken from soul to soul, in terms that avoid control by the intellect in a manner that is almost voluptuous." Noting that he threw himself and his hunger into communicating on film his "fantasies, outbursts of madness, neuroses, the convulsions of faith, and downright lies," Bergman did not flatly deny that his films may have some importance. However, he did express the belief that while art as self-satisfaction can have its importance for the artist, he regarded art, not only cinema but literature, music, painting, theater, as lacking importance. Concerning the various arts Bergman said:

New mutations and combinations emerge and are destroyed; seen from the outside, the movement possesses a nervous vitality—the magnificent zeal of artists to project, for themselves and an increasingly distracted public, pictures of a world that no longer asks what they think or believe. On a few preserves artists are punished, art is regarded as dangerous and worth stifling or steering. By and large, however, art is free, shameless, irresponsible and, as I said, the movement is intense, almost feverish; it resembles, it seems to me, a snakeskin full of ants. The snake itself is long since dead, eaten out from within, deprived of its poison; but the skin moves, filled with busy life.

If I now observe that I happen to be one of these ants, then I must ask myself whether there is any reason to pursue the activity further. The answer is yes.[7]

Having noted all that detracts from the importance of art, and that religion and art are kept in existence for sentimental reasons, Bergman revealed why, in spite of everything, he continued as an artist:

This reason is *curiosity*. An unbounded never satisfied, continuously renewed, unbearable curiosity, which drives me forward, never leaves me in peace, and completely replaces my past hunger for fellowship.

I feel like a prisoner who has served a long sentence and suddenly tumbled out into the booming, howling, snorting world outside. I am seized by an intractable curiosity. I note, I observe, I have my eyes with me, everything is unreal, fantastic, frightening, or ridiculous. I capture a flying particle of dust, perhaps it's a film—and of what importance will that be: none whatsoever, but I *myself* find it interesting, so it's a film. I revolve with the objects I have captured for myself and am cheerfully or melancholically occupied. I elbow my way in with the other ants, we do a colossal job. The snakeskin moves.

This and this only is *my* truth. I don't ask that it should be true for anyone else and, as comfort for eternity, it is naturally on the slim side.

As a basis for artistic activity during the next few years it is entirely adequate, at least for me.

To be an artist for one's own sake is not always very agreeable. But it has one outstanding advantage: the artist is on an equal footing with every other creature who also exists solely for his own sake. Taken together, we are probably a fairly large brotherhood who exist in this way in selfish fellowship on the warm, dirty earth, under a cold and empty sky.[8]

A careful reading of Bergman's statement should be coupled with a reading of his statement about his aim as a film-maker. He said:

People ask what are my intentions with my films—my aims. It is a difficult and dangerous question, and I usually give an evasive answer: I try to tell the truth about the human condition, the truth as I see it. This answer seems to satisfy everyone, but it is not quite correct. I prefer to describe what I *would like* my aim to be.

There is an old story of how the cathedral of Chartres was struck by lightning and burned to the ground. Then thousands of people came from all points of the compass, like a giant procession of ants, and together they began to rebuild the cathedral on its old site. They worked until the building was completed—master builders, artists, laborers, clowns, noblemen, priests, burghers. But they all remained anonymous, and no one knows to this day who built the cathedral of Chartres.

Regardless of my own beliefs and my own doubts, which are unimportant in this connection, it is my opinion that art lost its basic creative drive the moment it was separated from worship. It severed an umbilical cord and now lives its own sterile life, generating and degenerating itself. In former days the artist remained unknown and his work was to the glory of God. He lived and died without being more or less important than other artisans: "eternal values," "immortality" and "masterpiece" were terms not applicable in his case. The ability to create was a gift. In such a world flourished invulnerable assurance and natural humility . . .

Thus if I am asked what I would like the general purpose of my films to be, I would reply that I want to be one of the artists in the cathedral on the great plain. I want to make a dragon's head, an angel, a devil—or perhaps a saint—out of stone. It does not matter which; it is the sense of satisfaction that counts. Regardless of whether I believe or not, whether I am a Christian or not, I would play my part in the collective building of the cathedral.[9]

These two statements provide the key ingredients to under-standing not only Bergman's depiction of artists in all his films but to Bergman's understanding of the function and meaning of art in the contemporary world. Of course a very important part of that understanding includes his self-image and self-justification as an artist.

Crucial to Bergman's understanding of art is its severance from religion. At one time art received its power from the vision of the world created by religion. Because of the meaning that religion provided artists could spend years, indeed their entire lives, laboring anonymously on some work of art because they believed that this creation fit meaningfully into the scheme of creation, the artistic product brought forth by God's will. But for many artists today, religion is meaningless—some cling to it only for sentimental reasons. Thus art has lost its roots and its *raison d'être.* The artists cling to the ritual, the production of works that would be a real contribution in the world that religious belief affirmed, but now the ritual has lost its meaning and power. Bergman justifies his continuing to function as an artist by appealing to his curiosity. But of course he observes that art does have some power, that there still is some magic that can be conjured up. What is missing is the ultimate significance that art had in a God-centered-world.[10] With no Divine Father the only quasi-community that can be found is a strange brotherhood of people, each of whom lives for his or her own sake. As Bergman says this is a "selfish fellowship." The pessimism and sadness articulated in Bergman's statements should not be minimized.[11] Bergman is giving an ultimate view of art, an articulation of the ultimate significance or lack of significance of art.[12] But in spite of its loss of ultimate meaning, art for Bergman paradoxically is a key way of communicating with others. He has said of his work:

Every second in my pictures is made to move the audience.[13]

It's a conversation between me and the audience. It's a sort of contact. I want to get into contact with other people and my way of getting into contact with other people is my pictures.[14]

As we shall see in the next chapter, if there is a redemption or salvation it is through human communication. Of course one of the dimensions of Bergman's communication through art is to convey that art can not provide a resolution of life's problems. Livingstone has noted:

Bergman's supposed demonic quality springs from his rejection of blinding conventions that are at once aesthetic and social. Traditionally the artist, charged to imitate crises and their resolution before the eyes of the community, has found a role in this ritual, but this tradition is no longer tenable for Bergman, who would substitute for this mode of exchange between artist and audience a more difficult and constructive form of communication. He appears to be demonic because he probes the real crises that have disrupted so many aspects of contemporary culture, and because he asks his spectators to follow him in this exploration without offering them the guarantee of a reassuring conclusion.[15]

Bergman might be described as having a love-hate relation-ship with his craft. On the one hand, he can speak of film-making in what seem like very derogatory terms; but on the other hand he has been effusive in his awe of the powers of the camera. For example, an especially self-deprecating remark is the following:

When I show a film I'm guilty of deceit. I employ an apparatus constructed on a physical imperfection of man, an apparatus with which I cause in my public powerful shifts of emotion, like the swing-ing of a pendulum. I can make them laugh, scream with terror, smile, believe in legends, become indignant, shocked, seduced, or yawn with boredom. I am, then, either a deceiver or—when the public is aware of the deception—a performer of tricks. . . . This fact awakens, or should awaken, an unsolvable moral conflict in those who are occupied with making or selling the film industry's products.[16]

If this statement was Bergman's only word about cinema there would seem to be no point in continuing as a creator of films. The artist depicted in these remarks is nothing more than a very clever charlatan. The following statement conveys some-thing of the enthusiasm that we would expect from an artist who has created so many masterpieces.

I have an enormous need to influence other people, to touch other people both physically and mentally, to communicate with them. Mov-ies, of course, are a fantastic media [sic] with which to touch other human beings, to reach them, either to annoy them or to make them happy, to make them sad or get them to think.[17]

One of the themes that appears throughout the corpus of Bergman's films and is very much a part of his view of art, as well

Bergman creating art with cameraman Sven Nykvist.

as relationships, is the theme of humiliation. In an interview Bergman elaborated about how much humiliation has been a constant of his life.[18] Pointing out that one of the strongest memories of his childhood was being humiliated by words, acts or situations, Bergman remarked that not only are children often humiliated by grownups, but they too spend a good deal of their time humiliating one another. Claiming that the whole of education was one long humiliation, Bergman admitted that not only negative reviews of his work, but even laudatory reviews can be humiliating. Even depending on co-workers or others in the film or theater world was humiliating. The whole social structure, the bureaucracy and even Christianity cause humiliation. Bergman said:

If I've objected strongly to Christianity, it has been because Christianity is deeply branded by a very virulent humilation motif. One of its main tenets is "I, a miserable sinner, born in sin, who have sinned all my days, etc." Our way of living and behaving under this punishment is completely atavistic. I could go on talking about this humiliation business for ever. It's one of the big basic experiences. I react very strongly to every form of humiliation; and a person in my situation, in my position, has been exposed to whole series of real humiliations. Not to mention having humiliated others![19]

Bergman said that he knew exactly why artists feel humiliated. In fact, there is one instance in which he admits he took criticism that had been leveled against him and wrote it into one of his character's description of an artist. He says the feeling was liberating.[20] The criticism appears in *Through a Glass Darkly*, in Martin's criticism of David, his novelist father-in-law. Martin indicts David for not caring about the seriously ill Karin, David's daughter and Martin's wife.

MARTIN: You—love! In your emptiness there's no room for feelings, and as for any sense of decency, you just haven't got it. You know how everything should be expressed. At every moment you have the right word. There's only *one* phenomenon you haven't an inkling of: life itself.

. . . .

MARTIN: You're cowardly and sloppy, but on one point you're almost a genius. At explaining things away and apologizing.

. . . .

MARTIN: Write your book! Maybe it'll give you what you long for more than anything else: a name as an author. Then your daughter won't have been sacrificed in vain. . . .

. . . .

MARTIN: You've got a god you flirt with in your novels, but I can tell you, both your faith and your doubt are equally unconvincing. What strikes one most is your monstrous inventiveness.[21]

Bergman entitled his autobiography *The Magic Lantern*. In *The Magician*, it is the magic lantern which provides a clue not only to the depiction of art and the artist in that film, but to Bergman's self-understanding of his role as artist. Max von Sydow, the star of *The Magician* (*The Face*), has commented: "The real thing Bergman has been thinking of in *The Face* is himself, the actor, the artist. Vogler's reactions when he is forced are like those of Bergman."[22]

At the end of *The Magician* the camera focuses on a swinging lantern. The lantern has been set in motion by the carriage carrying Vogler and his troupe toward the palace to perform for the king. Racing up a narrow road the carriage brushes the hanging lantern, causing it to swing. The music rises to a crescendo as the carriage races up the road, but the music stops abruptly and the camera focuses on the swinging lantern. As the lantern swings the camera remains stationary. Then the music bursts forth again to provide a flourishing finish to the film. But what can we make of the ending? The pendulum movement symbolizes the shifts, surprises and reversals that characterize the plot, setting and characters in the film. The swinging lantern calls attention to the magic lantern that the acting troupe has, a lantern that in turn calls attention to the other magic lantern, the camera that is at the source of the film. This final referral reveals *The Magician* to be also a self-reflective statement by Bergman about film-making.

On the shifts, surprises and reversals throughout the film, Paisley Livingstone's comments are quite good.[23] Especially interesting for our preoccupation in this chapter is the radical reversals evident in the two protagonists in the film, Vogler, the artist-magician, and Vergerus, the man of science. Vogler is a silent mysterious figure, who seems to possess special powers and whose bearded face strongly resembles paintings of Christ. But he is also an insecure charlatan hiding behind a false beard who has tricks, but no supernatural powers. In the film Dr. Vergerus describes him aptly:

First we have the idealistic *Doctor* Vogler who practices as a physician according to Mesmer's rather doubtful methods. Then we have a somewhat less than idealistic *magician* who arranges all kinds of hocus-pocus according to entirely homemade recipes. If I've grasped the facts correctly, the activities of the Vogler troupe range unscrupulously between these two extremes.[24]

But Vergerus' identity is also two-sided and less than secure. Though a self-proclaimed enlightened atheist, a man of science and image of all that is rational and comprehensible, Vergerus is fascinated with Vogler and lusts for Vogler's wife, Manda. The ambivalence of Vergerus' character is revealed in a conversation he has with Manda. First he says, "When you first came into the room, I immediately liked you. Your face, your silence, your natural dignity." But then seconds later, he adds that she "represents something which I most abhor."[25] At one point Vergerus roughly grabs Vogler by the throat to see if there is a physical cause for the magician's silence; later in the attic the men switch places and Vogler grabs Vergerus by the neck, frightening the doctor into thinking that the dead one has risen. Vogler and Vergerus represent two different positions: the one stands for magic, even superstition, the other for science. Livingstone comments:

Yet these two positions appear to be mutually determined, and the distinction between them is drawn into the oscillation and rendered unstable. Vergerus claims that he "has no prestige to defend" in confronting Vogler, but this is far from true. "Prestige," we recall, signified in the seventeenth century a conjuring trick, and is derived from the Latin, *prestigium,* meaning "illusion." The verb *praestringere* means to bind fast, to blind, dazzle, or fascinate. Vergerus may not be a prestidigitator, but Vogler is not the only illusionist here: the doctor indeed claims a certain prestige, and defends the illusion that the science of medicine gives him a wholly rational and complete knowledge of man. His premise is that nothing in reality defies explanation, for if this were not so it would be necessary to conceive of a God.[26]

As was mentioned the switching and reversal evident in the character of Vogler and Vergerus happen not only in the settings but also in the plot. The most striking and initially confusing reversal in the plot occurs at the end of the film. Suspense has been created throughout by the swinging back and forth of character and plot. At the end it seems as though Vogler has been defeated in being revealed as merely a trickster. Then suddenly the invitation comes to perform at the palace. The music blares on the soundtrack as the troupe in blazing sunlight goes off to the palace. As has been pointed out, the ending is a *deus ex machina.* But how else could a human god, which is the most an artist can be, appear?[27] We are left with the swinging lantern at the end of the film, a striking visual commentary by Bergman on film as magic, and also on himself as film artist. The magic lantern can do almost anything to us, as a viewing of *The Magician* with its shifting movement, characters, plot and moods illustrates. The swinging lantern may be interpreted as a question from artist to audience: what has been depicted in the film and what does it all mean, including the depiction itself?[28]

Several films could be used to illustrate Bergman's reflections on art and the artist. *Hour of the Wolf, Shame, Passion* and *Autumn Sonata* contain vivid and disturbing portrayals of artists. Each film as a work of art can have a powerful impact on a viewer, moving the viewer to experience a world in which art can not redeem us but can show us the chaos that exists when human beings fail to make meaningful, healing contact.

Though *Hour of the Wolf* is not about either art or the artist in the way that *Persona* and *The Rite* are, the main character, Johan Berg, is a painter. Early in the film he articulates at least part of Bergman's questioning about art's significance.

I call myself an artist for want of a better name. In my creative work there is nothing self-evident except compulsion. I have through no fault of my own been pointed out as something special, a calf with five legs, a monster. I have never fought for that position and I shall not fight to keep it. Oh yes, I have felt megalomania waft about my brow, but I think that I am immune. I have only to think for a moment about the complete insignificance of art in the world of men to cool off. But the compulsion is still there. Perhaps it is a sickness or a mania.[29]

In *Shame* two musicians, Jan and Eva, try to live apart from the rest of the world and remain politically uninvolved. Even when a civil war has rendered their profession obsolete they try to live happily on a desolate island.[30] Eva wants to have children because she wonders whether two alone can reach fulfillment. The war that is waging is mirrored in the warring relationship that develops between Jan and Eva. War seems to be an extension of the cruelty that can be present in interpersonal relationships. The artist is depicted in the film as ineffectual, but Bergman's film itself is anything but ineffectual. It is a brilliant anti-war statement.

In *Autumn Sonata* Charlotte is a renowned concert pianist who has been so preoccupied with her career that she has neglected her two daughters. When she decides to visit them for a few days, she seems incapable of feeling or expressing emotions except through her music. She says of herself: "Actually I was completely ignorant of everything to do with love: tenderness, contact, intimacy, warmth. Only through music did I have a chance to show my feelings."[31] Charlotte is similar to David in *Through a Glass Darkly:* their artistic ambitions vitiate their relationships with their children. Even though she has not seen her daughters in years, when Charlotte tries to justify the visit to herself, the only reason she comes up with is that her experience of emotion might help her to play better.[32] Once again, though the artist in the film fails as a human being, Bergman's dramatic depiction of her failure makes his film exceptionally moving and provocative.

The two films that seem to me to be Bergman's most detailed commentary on art and the artist are *Persona* and *The Rite.* The former film is a genuine masterpiece, so innovative and brilliant that it is to the history of cinema what Joyce's *Ulysses* is to the history of literature. Let us deal with *The Rite* first, a film that clearly is a dramatization of Bergman's views on the artist both causing humiliation and being humiliated.

The Rite vividly reveals Bergman's problematic: the ritual of art in a non-sacral world.[33] The opening shot is of a man sitting at a desk holding a magnifying glass. He turns the glass toward the viewer, and with this visual touch Bergman has directly involved us in the film. The man is a judge and he begins an interrogation of three members of a troupe of nightclub performers—*Les Riens.* Though there are several charges against them, the most important one involves the obscenity of one of their numbers, entitled "The Ritual." In these opening moments Bergman has cinematically posed the key question to us: what is the ritual of art?

In questioning each of the three actors separately the judge reveals strong curiosity about their personal lives and tries to humiliate them even to the point of raping the female, Thea (Ingrid Thulin). Here we have a reversal, similar to those that took place in *The Magician:* the accuser is at least as guilty as the accused.[34] When the three performers act out "The Ritual" for the judge, it turns out to be a violent act of retribution against him. The performance has religious overtones and in explaining its origin one of the actors, Hans, describes it: "A ritual game. An incantation. A formula. You yourself must have known this weakness, a sensual longing for humiliation."[35] Soon the judge is confessing his sins, his abuse of his office, his need to humiliate people. Thea drinks some wine that is referred to as blood and the judge is literally frightened to death. Bergman has commented about the film:

When the interpreter kills the viewer, we can say we've reached the acme of committed theatre. The rite isn't just what they do at the end. It's a sort of papier-mâché game, with markers and things, all sorts of hocus-pocus. The rite is the game the artist plays with his audience,

Thea (Ingrid Thulin), Albert (Anders Ek) and Hans (Gunnar Björnstrand) perform their ritual.

between the artist and society—all this hodge-podge of mutual humiliation and mutual need for one another. That's the ritual element.[36]

In the last shot of the film Thea turns her head toward the
camera. Both the opening shots and the closing shot of the film
directly involve the viewer: the magnifying glass directed at us
and Thea's sinister stare.

Though the ritual performance has external similarity to a
Catholic Mass, the closest reality to anything like a god in the
film are the artists. They are the priests in a secular age. The
impression given of the artists in the film is that they are trapped.
They long for transcendence but there is none for the unbeliever. They go through meaningless ritual that, no longer ani-
mated by the fire of religious faith, can not free them. At one
point in the film Hans articulates the frustration of the artist in a
nonreligious society:

Dear God, let me out of this prison, I no longer believe in what we're
doing. We're meaningless, disgusting, absurd. We're not relevant
anymore.[37]

Seconds later the camera frames him against a wall on which
hangs a poster of a chained bear, recalling the symbol of the
bear, also used in *The Seventh Seal,* as sacrificial victim.[38] Of
course there is no salvation for Hans or any artist in a world
devoid of ultimate meaning.

In the film the violence of the judge against the actors is
duplicated when the artists violently humiliate and attack him.
Bergman even duplicates the camera's view: first the camera
peers over the judge's shoulder at the artists as victims and then
the camera bears down on the judge. The judge's final plea to
the actors is a disturbing proclamation of one lonely person

speaking to a "brotherhood in selfish fellowship," to use Bergman's term from his Snakeskin speech:

I'm a person with a first and last name. I was born, raised, and educated. I have lived a number of days and slept a number of nights. I have felt joy, laughed, felt sorrow, and have wept. Disappointment, tenderness, love. All of that is together in me. When you hit me in the head, Mr. Fischer, you strike all of that. I admire your physical daring. Your hand hits my head, which burns. But at the same time you strike my memory, my human dignity. You have hit me and humiliated yourself.[39]

The judge's pathetic plea is fitting in a world in which ultimate meaning cannot be discovered. In such a world the judge's attempt at identifying himself is understandable: personal identity also loses stability in an unstable universe. This is one of the key themes in one of the truly great films in the annals of cinematic history, *Persona*.

I am completely sympathetic to Susan Sontag's comment in her excellent essay on *Persona* in which she says the "most skillful attempt to arrange a single, plausible anecdote out of the film must leave out or contradict some of its key sections, images and procedures."[40] What Sontag's comment can make us wary of is the claim that one inclusive, univocal interpretation of the film can be achieved. I don't think so. Not long ago I was involved in a discussion of *Persona* with twelve people, most of whom had seen the film more than once. Everyone had an interpretation of the film different at least in parts from my own. Yet I would be hard pressed to call any of the interpretations erroneous, because I think the film is so rich that it can be viewed on several levels, and each level produces an interpretation that is fairly consistent. I think that dividing the film into four sections can help us to get a handle on what Bergman is saying about art, and also on his brilliant use of cinema to depict the substance of his vision. *Persona* is an extraordinary joining of style and substance. The four sections are: a prologue in which Bergman presents pieces of cinema referring to his own career or his present preoccupations, a narrative section in which events are "really happening," a third highly imaginative and at times surreal section in which nothing is exactly what it on the surface seems to be, and an epilogue.

In discussing *Persona* Bergman said:

Well, while I was working on *Persona,* I had it in my head to make a poem, not in words but in images, about the situation in which *Persona* had originated. I reflected on what was important, and began with the projector and my desire to set it in motion. But when the projector was running, nothing came out of it but old ideas, the spider, God's lamb, all that dull old stuff. My life just then consisted of dead people, brick walls, and a few dismal trees out in the park.[41]

Bergman's statement about his life at that moment refers to time he spent in the hospital between *The Silence* and *Persona.* While in the hospital Bergman made believe that he was a little boy who had died but who was not allowed to be really dead.[42] Bergman, revealing his psychological outlook at that time, said:

I was in the hospital, the view out of the window was a chapel where they were carrying out the bodies of the dead, and I knew that house was full of dead people. Of course, I felt it inside me somewhere that the whole atmosphere was one of death, and I felt like that little boy. I was lying there, half dead, and suddenly I started to think of two faces, two intermingled faces, and that was the beginning, the place where it started.[43]

The little boy is a key part of the prologue to the film.

The title of the film comes from the Latin word for mask, the disguise by means of which an actor portrays a part. Bergman's film is telling us that to be an actor is to wear a mask, but because we are in a non-sacral world, a world whose ultimate meaning eludes us, personal identity lacks ontological stability. In the film the masks of the two protagonists crack under the pressure of human experience.

The plot of *Persona* is simple. Actress Elizabeth Vogler has stopped speaking while performing in a stage production of *Electra*. A psychiatrist (Margaretha Krook) sends her along with a nurse, Alma, to the psychiatrist's summer home so that the nurse can restore Elizabeth to health. At the end of the film the two women leave to return to their two roles as actress and nurse. It is through the relationship of these two women, and through his relationship to us that Bergman dramatizes his metaphysical probings.

In *Persona* the frequency of images dealing with repetition and reversal, fusion and fission, inversion and duplication, have led some critics to interpret the film in terms of doubling. Susan Sontag wrote:

The theme is that of doubling; and the variations are those that follow from its leading possibilities—duplication, inversion, reciprocal exchange, repetition. Once again, it would be a serious misunderstanding to demand to know exactly what happens in *Persona;* for what is narrated is only deceptively, secondarily, a "story" at all. It's correct to speak of the film in terms of the fortunes of two characters named Elizabeth and Alma who are engaged in a desperate duel of identities. But it is no less true, or relevant, to treat *Persona* as what might be misleadingly called an allegory: as relating the duel between two mythical parts of a single "person," the corrupted person who acts (Elizabeth) and the ingenuous soul (Alma) who founders in contact with corruption.[44]

I would add two points to Sontag's comment. The film's theme of doubling can be studied not only on the formal and psychological levels, but on the ontological level as well. And the film can be spoken of not only as a duel of identities between Elizabeth and Alma, or between two mythical parts of a single self, but as a cinematic depiction of the relationship between artist (Bergman) and audience (us).

The images that open *Persona* seem to be disconnected and immediately challenge the viewer to be aware that this film experience will be different. What the images have in common, I think, is that they call the viewer to reflect on the nature of film. The first shot in the film is of a completely dark screen.[45] It is upon this screen that Bergman is going to create his work of art. The screen fulfills the function that a curtain plays on stage: it separates audience from artifice, differentiating the real reality (us) from the artificial reality (the film).[46] The next shot, initially confusing, is of the ends of the carbon and tungsten rods in a 35mm projector. These two points of light grow more bright. The rods move closer together, the light increases until the lights merge, sparks fly out and the whole frame is filled with very bright light. As Bergman has said, film is light. Marilyn Johns Blackwell suggests that this amalgamation of these components prefigures the tension between Alma and Elizabeth which eventually leads to a pure blending—"everything" devoid of self.[47] I think this occurs in the third part of the film. The light itself will take on a persona in the very appearance of the film.

Following the merging of the rods and the bright light, the next several seconds of film show various shots of the mechanical apparatus that make the projecting of a film on the screen possible. Some of these shots are accompanied by noises on the soundtrack that are also connected to the mechanics of running a film through a projector. Eventually we see the leader of film and shortly after that some images appear on the screen. Black-

well is very good on the significance of all these initially confusing shots.

Bergman is showing us his external resource, the film medium and its
projection system; by stressing the technical and mechanistic nature of
his medium, he asks us to remain aware, even as we are seduced by the
real-seeming artifice of the film, of the mundane machines and materials on which it is based. By concentrating our attention on the film
projection process, Bergman compels us to contemplate the fixity of
the film artifact. Unlike dramas, which can be rendered in a wide
variety of ways, a film is a final, complete, and unchangeable product.
Bergman would remind us that we are observing a consciously manipulated artwork; we see the celluloid, but look through it, as it were, so
that finally we cease to see it and see instead the persona of the film.
The image becomes the persona of the artwork, as surely as the
celluloid is the film itself.[48]

Bergman continues the introductory montage with a variety of
images, some of which refer to moviemaking such as a Pathé
fragment, some to his previous work such as a fragment that
appeared in his 1949 film *Prison*, a shot of a spider suggesting
the spider-God in *Through a Glass Darkly*, a winterscape that
suggests *Winter Light*, and some that refer to the time he spent in
the hospital gazing out the window at the morgue. One of the
shots in the montage is of a child on what looks like a bier. There
is also a close-up of a woman's head upside down followed by a
cut and then the woman's eyes are wide open.[49] All of this is
calling our attention to the nature of film, and to the artist,
Bergman, who is creating the film, and indirectly to us who will
view the film.

The last section of the introductory montage focuses on the
boy we saw on the bier. In a series of shots we see the boy lying
on the bier, turning toward the camera, sitting up and looking

around, rolling over and pulling the sheet over his shoulders allowing his feet to stick out. Though he tries to cover his feet he is unsuccessful and so he sits up giving the impression that he cannot return to sleep. He puts on glasses and begins to read a book, *The Hero of Our Times*. The music changes and develops into an eerie electronic music. The boy looks around, sits up, the music stops and all is silence. He looks directly into the camera and putting out his hand and moving it back and forth blocks out parts of the image. The camera then cuts behind the boy and we see him with his hand outstretched reaching toward an image that is not clear. He is reaching toward a white screen. The image behind the screen eventually appears as a woman's face, actually two women because the image is alternating shots of Bibi Andersson and Liv Ullmann. The last image is a close-up of the boy looking directly into the camera. Then the camera cuts to the title *Persona*.

There are several possible interpretations of the identity of the boy.[50] It is the same boy who appeared in *The Silence* in which he also read *The Hero of Our Times*. It has been suggested that in *Persona* he represents Bergman, that he is the aborted child of Alma, that he is the child that Elizabeth did not want. While there is nothing blatantly false about any of these interpretations, I think it better to think of him as an embodiment of us, the audience, trying not only to understand Alma and Elizabeth but to understand Bergman's work of art and indeed the role of art in the contemporary world.

During the credits Bergman intercuts various images. Noting that the titles are accompanied by several strange sounds Blackwell points out the images for us:

Intercut with these noises are kinetic, tachistoscopic images of the characters in the drama, and shots of a variety of subjects—a cut from the vaudeville Pathé fragment, the wooded winterscape from earlier, a pair of lips shown sideways, a monk immolating himself. Bergman also intercuts the title cards, which are printed with a spindly but rounded script reminiscent of printing popular during the 1930s, with images of rocks on a seashore and a picture of what appears to be dense but scraggly and barren white branches over a pale gray background, although the image is so abstract that it might well function as a visual analogue for the blood vessels in an eye, or for human ganglia. Both Bibi Andersson and Liv Ullmann appear twice in the title sequence, once fully lit from the front, facing the camera and looking "normal," and once with a black scarf on and one side of the face darkened so that it is all but invisible. But it is the image of the boy which appears most frequently during this sequence, looking straight out at us, a technique which seems reflexive insofar as it may well be a reference to the filmmaker himself and his childish delight with the apparatus of film-making. Some of the images are immediately recognizable; some, such as the lips and branches, are not.[51]

Alma means soul in Spanish and Elizabeth in Hebrew means consecrated to God. Of course the only gods the actress is conse-crated to are art and herself.[52] There is polarization between the two women from the start of the narrative. Each plays a role: Elizabeth the role of an actress but now also the role of a mute refusing to speak; Alma the role of a nurse, the embodiment of which is her uniform. When we first see Alma we hear a voice-over explaining Elizabeth's condition and during the voice-over we have a close-up of Elizabeth on stage. At the end of the voice-over we see Alma like a little uniformed school girl standing in front of the psychiatrist who is explaining Elizabeth's case to her. When Alma visits her new patient in her hospital room she identi-fies herself and tells about her background. In the next scene Alma tells the psychiatrist that she doubts whether she is up to the job of helping Elizabeth, that she does not possess the "great spiritual strength." We then have a scene in which Alma is fussing about Elizabeth's room and turns on the radio for the patient. Elizabeth laughs heartily as she hears the following:

Forgive me, forgive me darling, you have to forgive me. All I want is your forgiveness. Forgive me so that I can breathe again—and live again. What do you know of mercy, what do you know of a mother's suffering, the bleeding pain of a woman? Oh God, God, somewhere out there in the darkness that surrounds us all. Look in mercy upon me. Thou who art love.

Confused by Elizabeth's laughter Alma says:

Though I do have a tremendous admiration for artists and I think art is tremendously important in life—particularly for people who are in some kind of difficulty.[53]

Between Elizabeth and Alma we have two different views of art: one view that art is so fake that it is laughable and not even worthy of involvement, the other that it is something very important in life. *Persona* is about these two views.

One of the most revealing coupling of scenes in the film happens early on when Bergman shows the two women during the night, Alma restless in her bed unable to sleep and Elizabeth pacing in her hospital room with the only light coming from the screen of the television set. Alma is talking to herself, trying to reassure herself about the stability and orderliness of her life, that she will marry, have children and live a normal live. No matter how she tries to calm herself, even with one of the sleeping tablets, which significantly are right by her bed, she cannot sleep. As Elizabeth is pacing she sees a scene on a news program covering the Vietnam War. She sees a Buddhist priest protesting by burning himself to death. Bergman's cinematic skill is very evident here. He cuts between the monk and Eliza-

Alma (Bibi Andersson) unable to sleep because of her unresolved conflicts.

beth, drawing the action into close-up. He even shows the same footage of the monk twice to underline its horror. The scene of Alma suggests her ordered life is a facade; the scene of Elizabeth suggests her silent withdrawal is connected to the meaninglessness of life, evident through the extraordinary cruelty that can infect human relationships.

When Elizabeth receives a letter from her husband she has Alma read it to her. The pleas of her husband for more intimacy seem to so move Elizabeth to anger that she tears the enclosed photo of her son in half. In the next scene Elizabeth is with the psychiatrist who articulates the central problem of the film. She tells Elizabeth that she understands the actress' problem and why she has chosen to remain mute:

The hopeless dream of *being*. Not doing, just being. Aware and watchful every second. And at the same time the abyss between what you are for others and what you are for yourself. The feeling of dizziness and the continual burning need to be unmasked. At last to be seen through, reduced, perhaps extinguished. Every tone of voice a lie, an act of treason. Every gesture false. Every smile a grimace. The role of wife, the role of friend, the roles of mother and mistress, which is worst? Which has tortured you most? Playing the actress with the interesting face? Keeping all the pieces together with an iron hand and getting them to fit? Where did it break? Where did you fail? Was it the role of mother that finally did it? It certainly wasn't your role as *Electra*. That gave you a rest. She actually got you to hold out a while more. She was an excuse for the more perfunctory performances you gave in your other roles, your "real-life roles." But when *Electra* was over, you had nothing left to hide behind, nothing to keep you going. No excuses. And so you were left with your demand for truth and your disgust. Kill yourself? No—too nasty, not to be done. But you could be immobile. You can keep quiet. Then at least you're not lying. You can cut yourself off, close yourself in. Then you don't have to play a part, put on a face, make false gestures. Or

Elizabeth listens silently to the doctor's explanation of her silence.

so you think. But reality plays tricks on you. Your hiding place isn't watertight enough. Life starts leaking in everywhere. And you're forced to react. No one asks whether its genuine or not, whether you're true or false. It's only in the theatre that's an important question. Hardly even there, for that matter. Elizabeth, I understand that you're keeping quiet, not moving, that you have put this lack of will into a fantastic system. I understand it and admire you for it. I think you should keep playing this part until you've lost interest in it. When you've played it to the end, you can drop it as you drop your other parts.[54]

Kawin points out that Elizabeth's search for being is analogous to the photograph's attempt to become unfiltered, undefined light.[55] I think Elizabeth's desire is an expression of Bergman's desire to artistically depict reality as it is, to be accurately and profoundly objective.

When the two women go to the beach there are pleasant shots of them walking on the beach, sitting side by side sorting mushrooms and sunning themselves. At the beach there is another rather important piece of dialogue. Alma is reading and decides to read aloud a section of her book to Elizabeth. As she reads the section the camera shoots five different desolate rockscapes and then cuts to alternating shots of the faces of Alma and Elizabeth. The text read aloud which Alma disagrees with, but which Elizabeth affirms is:

All the anxiety we bear with us, our disappointed dreams, the inexplicable cruelty, our terror at the thought of extinction, the painful insight we have into the conditions of life on earth, have slowly crystallized out our hope of heavenly salvation. The great shout of our faith and doubt against the darkness and silence is the most terrifying evidence of our forlornness, our terrified unexpressed knowledge.[56]

The remainder of the film will depict the accuracy of Elizabeth's belief while revealing the disintegration of Alma's faith.

The women become sufficiently close that Alma confesses an affair with a married man and an orgy she engaged in with some teenage boys. At the end of the confession, Alma, weeping and terribly confused about her guilt feelings, puts her face in her hands and the screen goes completely black, a good visual metaphor for Alma's confusion and despair.[57]

The next two scenes raise questions that are not easy to answer. Elizabeth and Alma are sitting at a table at night and Alma wearily puts her head on the table. A voice says: "You should go to bed. Otherwise you will fall asleep here at the table." Alma raising her head sleepily says: "I should go to bed. Otherwise I'll fall asleep here at the table."[58] During the night Elizabeth enters Alma's room and the two look into the camera as Elizabeth pushes back Alma's hair and slowly puts her mouth on Alma's neck. The next day Alma asks Elizabeth whether she spoke and whether she entered Alma's room. Elizabeth denies doing either. Did she? Though arguments could be offered for several possible explanations I think what is key is the confusion that is caused in the viewer. As Alma and Elizabeth are losing their identities, we are losing cognitive control of the work of art.

In the next scene Bergman reminds us that we are the audience viewing a film when he has Elizabeth look right at us and photograph us. Rather than destroy our illusion, this makes us more attentive to the film. Bergman has said:

If one jerks the audience out of the action for a moment and then lures it back, one increases its sensibility and receptivity instead of diminishing it.[59]

In the scenes in which Elizabeth apparently speaks, visits Alma's bedroom at night and photographs us, we experience disorientation. The film seems to be escaping from us.

Later Alma, going to mail a letter that Elizabeth has written,

Alma and Elizabeth have their mystical middle of the night meeting.

Elizabeth taking our picture as Bergman tries to jerk us out of the
action and so increase our sensibility.

reads the letter. In the letter Elizabeth patronizingly speaks of how amusing Alma is. Alma is hurt deeply and desires revenge. Back at the house she accidentally breaks a glass on the stone pavement. Knowing that Elizabeth is walking barefoot, Alma leaves one piece of glass on the pavement and waits for Elizabeth to step on it. Alma watches from the window as Elizabeth winces in pain as she steps on the glass. The women's eyes meet and Elizabeth realizes what Alma has done. With Alma in close-up the film splits down the middle, dividing her face in two, then rejoins and then seems to burn. It is as though the film burns from so much cruelty, as though the film itself can not bear the weight of this cruelty.[60] With this striking device Bergman once again reminds us that we are watching a film. So ends the second part of the film, most of which follows a normal narrative pattern with subtle camera work.

The third part of the film does not seem to follow a normal narrative pattern. Is it a dream? If so, whose? The third part of the film seems to be depicting a breakdown in personal identity. At one point Alma is so furious with Elizabeth's silence that she shakes her and in retaliation Elizabeth slaps Alma and bloodies her nose. Furious, Alma grabs a pot of boiling water and approaches the actress who screams "No, stop it." Their physical fighting is so filmed that we seem to be in the midst of it. After frightening Elizabeth Alma says:

Well, at least you were frightened. Weren't you? For a few seconds you may have been absolutely honest. An honest fear of death. Alma's gone mad, you thought. What sort of person are you really? Or did you only think "I'll remember that face. That expression. That tone of voice."[61]

Later when Alma is chasing Elizabeth along the beach pleading for forgiveness Alma seems to be asking for forgiveness and then answering her own questions. The fusion of the two personalities seems to be happening. These pleas of Alma are taking place along the same rocks on which Alma earlier in the film had read the despairing message from the book. The barren rocks are a fitting sign of the spiritual and emotional landscapes of despair at which Alma has arrived.[62]

Later we see Elizabeth in her room looking at a photograph of a child in Warsaw being taken off by Nazi soldiers. The child's face registers confusion. Once again we are struck by the unbearable cruelty that people inflict on one another. Robin Wood notes:

The relationship between the photograph of a public outrage and the psychic cruelty between the two women is very interesting: each has the effect, in a different way, of universalizing the significance of the other.[63]

The next segment of film shows Alma entering Elizabeth's room at night and berating the sleeping actress. While Alma is doing this we hear a voice offscreen calling "Elizabeth." What follows seems to be a dream. Alma meets Elizabeth's husband in the woods. Elizabeth is also present. Alma tells the husband that she is not Elizabeth, but with Elizabeth present they seem to make love. Elizabeth is present throughout observing and listening to them. Though for a time Alma seems to act as though she is Elizabeth, she finally cries: "Give me an anaesthetic. Throw me away. I can't, I can't go on. Leave me alone. It's shameful. Leave me alone. I'm cold, rotten and indifferent."[64] There is an extreme close-up of Elizabeth and the screen goes white. Blackwell notes that in this dream or fantasy Alma is trying to usurp part of Elizabeth's character but Alma's form of revenge backfires—in trying to humiliate Elizabeth by seducing her husband Alma herself is humiliated.[65]

The next scene suggests that Elizabeth's absorption of Alma

becomes complete. The scene opens with Elizabeth's hand hiding something on a table. Alma sees that it is a photograph of Elizabeth's son and says that they must talk about this.

With the camera on Elizabeth's face we hear a monologue by Alma in which she indicts Elizabeth for being such a poor parent. At the end of the monologue the whole scene begins again. Alma gives the same monologue but this time the camera is on her face. The dual monologue sequence is concluded with a closeup of a face, the left half of the picture is Alma's face, the right half is Elizabeth's face. In a sense Alma's monologue also applies to Alma because she aborted a child. The Elizabeth side of the close-up goes into complete darkness and Alma cries "No, I am not you. I don't feel like you. I'm Sister Alma. I'm just here to help you. I'm not Elizabeth Vogler. You are Elizabeth Vogler. I want. I love. I don't have."[66] Alma is trying to recapture her identity but it is impossible. The composite image returns and then the screen fades to white.

Bergman fills the last moments of his film with haunting images all of which underline the loss of identity that Alma has experienced. At one point there is even babble spoken by Alma to suggest this loss of identity. In one surreal shot Elizabeth sucks blood from Alma's arms. In another scene Alma says to Elizabeth "Repeat after me: Nothing." Elizabeth says "Nothing" and Alma replies "That's it. That's right. That's how it will be."

One of the more striking images in the final moments is of Alma as the women are preparing to leave the summer home to return to their roles as actress and nurse. As Alma looks in the mirror and strokes her hair off her forehead there is another faint image in the mirror of Elizabeth stroking the hair off Alma's forehead.

Several images in the closing moments of the film call our attention back to the beginning of the film. Alma leaves the summer house suitcase in hand. There is a closeup of Elizabeth in her Electra makeup. There is also a shot of Bergman and cinematographer Sven Nykvist high up on a crane. We can see in their camera an upside-down shot of Elizabeth that has not appeared previously in this film and which may refer to a new film on which Bergman is working. Alma boards a bus and as it departs the camera focuses on the gravel and we see a superimposition of the boy from the morgue trying to touch the face he was trying to touch at the beginning of the film. The image dissolves totally into that of the boy in the morgue trying to touch the face of the woman. Then the screen goes white and this is replaced by a shot of the film running off its spool out of the projector. Then we see the white screen again and it dissolves into the two arcs of light which then slowly are extinguished and *Persona* has ended. It is fitting that the two arcs of light that end the epilogue are the two arcs of light which started the prologue.

Persona is a movie masterpiece that beautifully illustrates Bergman's view of art. In a world in which God, religion and the sacred no longer have significant meaning art assumes a special importance. However, according to Bergman's love-hate view of art, the artist is in a no-win situation. When art and the artist were inspired by God, religion and the sacred, art had a special significance. Even to make a small contribution to the building of a cathedral was to make a significant contribution. In today's world art can have no such significance. Elizabeth's "Nothing" can be taken as an evaluation of art's importance. However, though complete success is impossible, artists feel they must continue to create, continue to try to produce something of significance. In a radically meaningless world they cannot succeed. The transitory contact and communication with others, which can be a sign of love and concern, is the only achievement open to artists. As an attempt at communication art is one way of battling the inevitable destination of every person, death.

6

Love: The Only Salvation Available

THERE IS NO single topic that so ties together all of Bergman's films as the topic of love. There are numerous themes in Bergman's work—some of those themes are developed in detail in a particular film and only touched on in another—but no theme is so consistently present nor so illuminating of all of Bergman's work as the theme of loving communication between people. In film after film it takes center stage. Even Bergman's preoccupation with death and with religious symbols can best be understood in terms of the ability or inability of human beings to touch one another in love. In order to fully understand the search for meaning, the problem of death and the problem of God's silence, these themes have to be seen in light of the Swedish director's belief that people have enormous difficulty in communicating lovingly. Even Bergman's mixed feelings toward the vocation of the artist can be illuminated through reflection on his view of love.

When the knight sitting on the beautiful hillside at sunset receives the strawberries and milk from Jof and Mia and announces that the memory of this experience "will be an adequate sign—it will be enough for me" he is announcing that love is the hope that people have as they face the sufferings of life and especially the suffering of death. The love between Jof and Mia will encourage the knight as he continues his battle with death. Earlier in the film when Jof and Mia are talking outside the wagon that carries their costumes and other belongings, Bergman visually expresses how their love somehow conquers death. He films them standing in front of the wagon. In the background we can see that hanging on the side of the wagon is a mask of death. In the face of the love between Jof and Mia death is reduced to a hollow mask.

It is no accident that only Jof and Mia and their child escape from Death in the film. All the others making the journey with the knight are taken by Death. Saving Jof and Mia becomes the one significant act that the knight performs, the one act that enables him to face death and yet affirm some meaning. After the scene on the hillside, the knight smilingly resumes the game of chess with Death. When Death asks why he is laughing, the knight comments that the game amuses him. Having experienced the love between Jof and Mia, the knight has a new perspective on death. However, the knight stops smiling when Death asks "Are you going to escort the juggler and his wife through the forest? Those whose names are Jof and Mia and who have a small son."[1] The knight realizes that Death plans to take them too. Later in the chess game the knight distracts Death so that Jof and Mia can escape. In Bergman's vision, death cannot conquer love.

The whole point of Dr. Isak Borg's journey through memory in *Wild Strawberries* is to highlight for him and us the closedness and coldness that have characterized his life. The clock with no hands in Borg's dream early in the film suggests that the doctor's time is running out. Unless he loves someone, his physical death will just be the physical counterpart of the emotional and spiritual death he underwent years previously. The experience of death will be especially tragic if death snuffs out a life in which there was no love.

In one sense, the plot of *Wild Strawberries* covers one day in

the life of Isak Borg; in another sense it covers five generations
of the Borg family.[2] On Dr. Borg's trip to Lund to receive his
award, he stops by to see his mother who tells him about her
mother. Dr. Borg has as his traveling companion his daughter-
in-law Marianne (Ingrid Thulin), who is pregnant. The story of
the Borg family, up to and including Dr. Borg's son Evald
(Gunnar Björnstrand), has been a story of coldness and aloof-
ness. There seems to be little love among the Borgs. At the time
of the journey to Lund, Marianne is having serious marital
difficulties with Evald, who feels cut off and unloved by his
father. Through dreams and flashbacks we discover that Dr.
Borg, when he was a young man, lost the girl he wished to marry,
Sara (Bibi Andersson), because of his incapacity for warmth and
tenderness.

On the trip toward Lund Marianne's dislike of the doctor
becomes so evident that he finally asks her to be honest and tell
him what she has against him. Marianne replies:

You are an old egotist, Father. You are completely inconsiderate and
you have never listened to anyone but yourself. All this is well hidden
behind your mask of old-fashioned charm and your friendliness. But
you are hard as nails, even though everyone depicts you as a great
humanitarian. We who have seen you at close range, we know what you
really are. You can't fool us. For instance, do you remember when I
came to you a month ago? I had some idiotic idea that you would help
Evald and me. So I asked to stay with you for a few weeks. Do you
remember what you said?[3]

After the doctor claims that he said that she was most cor-
dially welcome, Marianne says:

This is what you really said, but I'm sure you've forgotten: Don't try to
pull me into your marital problems because I don't give a damn about
them, and everyone has his own troubles.[4]

The flashbacks and dreams that are sprinkled throughout the film confirm Marianne's accusation. Early in the film we see that Borg cannot even relate in warmth to Agda (Jullan Kindahl) who has been the family maid for decades. However by the end of the film Borg has seen his problems with a new clarity. Having confronted his death and the lovelessness of his life he begins to reach out to people. He tries to communicate in a new way with Agda, Evald and Marianne. There is a tentative success with each. The final dream in the film reveals that Borg has achieved a certain peace by understanding his self-centeredness and by trying in the little time left to him to do something about it. In the final dream Borg is looking for his mother and father, but he can't find them. His childhood sweetheart Sara tells him she will help him and leads him to the edge of a narrow sound. He sees his parents on the other side—his father fishing, his mother sitting by the bank. They see Isak. The father laughingly waves and the mother laughs and nods toward her son. His parents' acceptance of him marks a kind of a new birth for Isak. At seventy-six, Borg has come to life because he has begun to love.

The primary metaphor for loving communication in *Cries and Whispers* is speech. Most of the characters in the film do not successfully communicate with one another. In the face of death speech becomes either a screaming cry of pain from cancer or an inaudible whisper. Maria cannot relate maturely, either to her husband or to her lover, the doctor. Karin is so cold and closed that she can relate to no one. She hates her husband, and except for the brief loving encounter with Maria which we referred to in the chapter on death, she refuses to open herself to Maria. Karin has come to believe life is a matrix of lies. In the opening seconds of the scene in which she cuts herself, she and her husband are having dinner. With little dialogue, but with good camerawork, cutting and fine acting, the viewer receives in a matter of seconds an overwhelming impression of a relationship that is worse than dead: husband and wife hate one another. Ingrid Thulin conveys a kind of nervous contempt, presumably because she knows that in moments she will share a bed with the man she despises; the husband conveys a confident dominance, presumably because he plans to sexually humiliate and dominate this woman who detests him. The few moments are a frightening but powerful phenomenology of a sado-masochistic relationship. When Karin goes into her dressing room to prepare for bed, Anna tries to help her. Then like the sailor-captain in the lifeboat at the end of *Shame,* Karin can't stand Anna's presence or her stare. Karin slaps her. The impression that Bergman suggests is very reminiscent of Sartre's claim—"Hell is other people." Human relationships can become so strained that people can't tolerate the presence of one another. After slapping her, Karin asks Anna to forgive her. Silent, Anna shakes her head indicating her refusal to forgive.

The only two people in the film who seem to be able to relate in love are Agnes and Anna.[5] In the film we discover that Agnes had been kind to Anna and to Anna's small child before the child died. Now Anna is the only one whose love for Agnes is sufficiently strong to comfort her as Agnes faces death. The surrealistic scene near the end of the film in which Agnes' corpse calls to the three women highlights the strength of the love between Agnes and Anna. When Anna embraces the corpse Bergman makes his point that somehow love conquers even death.

Yet in Bergman's universe love is never completely secure. Loving communication seems a fragile event that takes place in precarious surroundings. Love is always threatened. Passing moments of love may be all for which we can hope. It is in light of this that I think the final scene of *Cries and Whispers* should be intrepreted. As Anna is reading Agnes' diary and we hear Agnes' voice on the soundtrack, Bergman cuts to a lovely summer scene. The four women are dressed in white. Their surround-

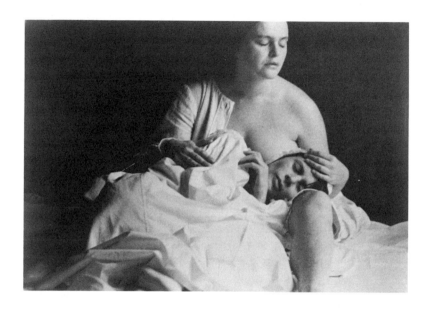

Anna (Kari Sylwan) holds the dead body of Agnes (Harriet
Andersson) in a *Pietà*-like pose in *Cries and Whispers*.

ings are the lush green of the family estate. They seem happy. On the soundtrack Agnes' voice says that "Come what may, this is happiness" and that she feels a great gratitude for what her life has given her. And then the screen goes red and Bergman announces "And so the cries and whispers fade away." Some critics have interpreted this last scene as irony and cynicism.[6] They believe that because of Karin's frigidity and Maria's immaturity, no real deep love ever existed among the sisters. Though Agnes may have loved her sisters they both were incapable of anything resembling love. And so the final scene would make Agnes' death even more of a tragedy because she was so deceived even during her life. I disagree with the intrepretation. Certainly Karin and Maria are not outgoing, giving, loving people. But in Bergman's world, few people are. Yet even a selfish, self-centered person may be able to make some loving contact occasionally and for a brief time. I think this is what the end of the film is saying: Agnes has experienced the love from Anna and also from Maria and Karin in their weak imperfect way, and this experience of love makes life of some value. This type of experience of love prevents life from being "sound and fury signifying nothing." Any experience of love, however weak, makes the cries and whispers fade away.

In *Face to Face* the battle between love and death is underlined by the symbols of the flower-window and the woman with the enlarged eye. After Jenny attempts suicide we learn through her dreams that she did not receive sufficient love during her early years, and that in her adult life she is unable to give love. Jenny's conflict, very dramatically portrayed, is the basic problem of every person. As her friend Dr. Tomas Jacobi is trying to comfort her in the hospital, he engages in a conversation with Jenny that reveals that her situation is just a dramatic example of the human situation. Everyone is in essentially the same spot as Jenny. She asks him:

Do you think I'm crippled for the rest of my life? Do you think we're a vast army of emotionally crippled wretches wandering about calling to each other with words which we don't understand and which only make us even more afraid?[7]

Admitting that he doesn't know, Jacobi tells her that there is an incantation, a kind of a prayer that unbelievers can say. When asked by her what it is, Jacobi says:

I wish that someone or something would affect me *so that I can become real.* I repeat over and over: Let me become real one day.

Jenny asks what he means by real and he responds:

To hear a human voice and be sure that it comes from someone who is made just like I am. To touch a pair of lips and in the thousandth of a second know that this is a pair of lips. Not to have to live through the hideous moment needed for my experience to check that I've really felt a pair of lips. Reality would be to know that a joy is a joy and above all that a pain is a pain.[8]

The only way to become real in Bergman's world is through loving communication. After the ordeal of her attempted suicide and the surrealistic depiction of her problems through her four dreams, Bergman has Jacobi, who is acting as her physician, tell Jenny she can leave the hospital. The dismissal suggests that her problem is no different from that of every other human being, except that Jenny's existential situation reached a crisis point. Jacobi's parting words to Jenny suggest the one medicine that may help the "vast army of emotionally crippled wretches." He says "Bye-bye. Take care of yourself and those who are fond of you."[9]

After Jenny returns to her grandparents' home, as she sees her grandparents' concern for one another, she makes a discovery: "For a moment I saw that love embraces all, even death." Jenny's insight suggests both the triumph of love and the tentativeness of love's triumph. Jenny may slip back into her unloving ways but at least for a moment she saw that love can confront death. Her calling of the hospital and her announcement that she will be at work the next day suggest that she has gained enough insight into the human predicament to try to continue. Bergman's cutting to the stained glass flower-window and having sunlight shine through it provides one of the more hopeful endings to a Bergman film.

Everything that has been said about love applies to *Shame*, not because Bergman's anti-war film illustrates the beauty of love but because it shows what the world would be like without love. In the war-torn country depicted in *Shame* there is no successful love relationship and so there really is no adequate response to death. The action of the sailor-captain sliding off the side of the boat at the end of the film makes as much sense as any other human action in an absurd world. Without love the Sartrean claim that "Hell is other people" is quite insightful.

The film opens with Jan mentioning that he's had a dream about playing in the orchestra. As we mentioned previously, the symphony orchestra suggests a totally ordered world. Just before the film ends Eva, sitting in the lifeboat, tells about a dream she has just had while she was asleep in the boat. It's a very sad dream. It involves the loss of something precious. She mentions that she has this feeling that she has forgotten something that she should have remembered. The viewer has the sense that whatever Eva has forgotten might be something that would make human existence of some value. In discussing the dream Bergman said:

Eva says: I had a feeling there was something I ought to have remembered, which I've forgotten. It's about the burning roses and the child she feels against her cheek. It's about everything that *is*—water, clear green running water, like a mirror. It's a dream I've had myself, a pure visual experience of something beautiful and delightful that has happened; something unattainable and which has been carelessly wasted. It must have something to do with love, I suppose.[10]

Probably the most direct way to get a handle on Bergman's view of love is to consider his trilogy *Through a Glass Darkly, Winter Light* and *The Silence.* Certainly the three films can be interpreted solely in terms of Bergman's view of God.[11] The material in the films as well as the subtitles of the films (*Through a Glass Darkly*—certainty achieved, *Winter Light*—certainty unmasked, *The Silence*—God's silence—the negative impression) lend themselves to this kind of interpretation. However, the interpretation Bergman offered is probably more on target. Though artists on occasion may be the worst interpreters of what they have done, in this case Bergman can be our guide. In discussing the trilogy Bergman said:

Each film, you see, has its moment of contact, of human communication: the line "Father spoke to me" at the end of *Through a Glass Darkly;* the pastor conducting the service in the empty church for Marta at the end of *Winter Light;* the little boy reading Ester's letter on the train at the end of *The Silence.* A tiny moment in each film—but the crucial one. What matters most of all in life is being able to make that contact with another human. Otherwise you are dead, like so many people today are dead. But if you can take that first step toward communication, toward understanding, toward love, then no matter how difficult the future may be—and have no illusions, even with all the love in the world, living can be hellishly difficult—then you are saved. This is all that really matters, isn't it?[12]

In *Through a Glass Darkly,* Bergman examines relationships among four characters: a father David, his son Minus and daughter Karin and her husband Martin. Bergman places these four characters on an island isolated from others. Karin's love for her husband is weak and the father seems disinterested in his two children.

Karin is suffering from a disease that will eventually lead to insanity. After David learns this from Martin he writes:

Her illness is hopeless, with occasional improvements. I have long suspected it, but the certainty, even so, is almost unbearable. To my horror, I note my own curiosity. The impulse to register its course, to note concisely her gradual dissolution. To make use of her.[13]

Karin finds the diary and reads what her father has written. When Martin discovers what she has read he confronts David with the lovelessness in David's life. The two men are out at sea in a rowboat. They seem to be adrift and the image is a good one to suggest the rootlessness of contemporary man. David tries to excuse what he has written about Karin in his diary by saying that he loves his daughter. Martin says:

You—love! In your emptiness there's no room for feelings, and as far as any sense of decency, you just haven't got it. You know how everything should be expressed. At every moment you have the right word. There's only *one* phenomenon you haven't an inkling of: life itself.[14]

After accusing him of just wishing to obtain a name as an author Martin has the following dialogue with David:

MARTIN: You've got a god you flirt with in your novels, but I can tell you, both your faith and your doubt are equally unconvincing. What strikes me most is your monstrous inventiveness.

David being confronted by Martin concerning his self-centeredness.

DAVID: Don't you think I know?

MARTIN: Well then. Why go on? Why don't you do something respectable for a living?

DAVID: What could I do?

MARTIN: Have you ever written so much as a true word in any of your books? Reply if you can.

DAVID: I don't know.

MARTIN: There! But the worst of it is your lies are so refined they resemble truth.

DAVID: I do my best.

MARTIN: Maybe. *But you never succeed.*

DAVID: I know.

MARTIN: You're empty and clever and now you think you'll fill your emptiness with Karin's extinction. The only thing I don't understand is how you fancy you can mix God up in all this. He must be more inscrutable than ever.[15]

In this scene there are references to a number of Bergman's favorite themes, such as the dishonesty and superficiality of the artist, the preoccupation with faith and doubt and the inscrutable God. But the most important point, the point upon which the scene is built, is Martin's indictment of David as being empty and unloving.

The relationships in the film reveal the weaknesses of the characters. Martin, a doctor, is ineffectual as he tries to comfort and heal Karin with his love. Minus, a typical adolescent struggling to find his self-identity, gawky and shy with girls, is bothered when his sister teases him in a kind of flirtatious way. Karin, in the process of losing her mind, eventually seduces her brother. The incest is a sign of the disordered world in which the four characters live. Karin also has a horrible apparition of God as a spider.

Bergman's view of love is contained in the final speech in the film when David confesses to Minus that he takes consolation in life from love, from all sorts of love, the "highest and the lowest, the poorest and the richest, the most ridiculous and the most sublime." At last David has communicated with his son. Bergman, perhaps correctly, has looked back on this film and been critical of it.[16] There does seem to be a gap between the ending and the rest of the film. The hope expressed at the end of the film doesn't seem to form a piece, an artistic whole with the pessimism expressed in the earlier parts of the film. In that sense the film doesn't have the unity that a great work of art should have. Yet the film's impact is enormous.

The Swedish title of *Winter Light* is *The Communicants,* and that suggests the central theme of the film. The minister Tomas is struggling with his faith. Bergman's brilliant opening scene of the communion service hints at what we come to discover as the film develops. Tomas is a healer who is more wounded than those to whom he is ministering. He is a person who is cold and aloof. The tragedy of Tomas for Bergman is not that he is losing his faith in God but that he has no faith in human love and seems incapable of either giving or receiving love.

Tomas' hope for salvation is Marta (Ingrid Thulin) who is a schoolteacher, an atheist and a loving, unselfish woman. Tomas' struggles with faith are basically meaningless to her. With a technique he was to use again with great effect in *Autumn Sonata* Bergman reveals the problems between Marta and Tomas through a letter that Marta writes to Tomas. Bergman has Tomas begin to read the letter but then cuts to Marta facing the camera and reciting the words of her letter. This cinematic device is quite powerful. The viewer has a much stronger sense of Marta's struggle to save Tomas by seeing and hearing Marta face to face. Also the viewing audience can get a sense of being spoken to, that *their* consciences are being prodded. In the letter Marta pinpoints Tomas' problem, and that problem is for Berg-

Pastor Tomas conducting a communion service for a handful of communicants.

man the human problem: the difficulty of loving communication.
Marta tells a long story concerning a serious attack of eczema
that made her hands and face unattractive. Reminding Tomas
that he had not thought to pray for her when she had the
eczema, she chides him in the letter for being repelled by her
unattractiveness. Then she facetiously tells him of a prayer, the
efficacy of which she doesn't believe in, because she is an
atheist. In the letter she tells Tomas she prayed as follows:

God, I said to myself, why have you created me so eternally dissatisfied, so frightened, so bitter? Why must I understand how wretched I
am, why have I got to suffer as in the hell of my own indifference? If
there is a purpose in my suffering, then tell me what it is! And I'll bear
my pain without complaining. I'm strong. You've made me so terribly
strong, both in body and soul, but you give me nothing to do with my
strength. Give me a meaning to my life, and I'll be your obedient
slave! . . . This autumn I've realized my prayer has been heard. And
here's your cue to laugh. I prayed for clarity of mind and I got it. I've
realised I love you. I prayed for a task to apply my strength to, and got
it, too. It's you.[17]

She then confesses in the letter that she loves Tomas and that
her one wish is to be able to live for him.
The struggle between Marta's love for Tomas and Tomas'
inability to love reaches its resolution at the end of the film.
Tomas has arrived at Frostnas for Vespers. Marta is in the back
of the church. She and the organist and the sacristan and Tomas
are the only people in the church. Tomas is in the sacristy talking
to the sacristan. In the back of the church, while waiting to find
out if Vespers is going to take place, the rather cynical organist
talks to Marta about Tomas. After predicting to her that there'll
be no service because there is no congregation present, he
comments that Tomas "has about as much knowledge of human

nature as my old galoshes." He mentions that the love relationship between Tomas and his wife, now dead, was a disaster. The organist cynically points out that Tomas worshiped her, showered all his love on her but that she was a completely cold and unfeeling woman. Then he says:

> That's what you can call love, if you like! Jesus! But it put an end to the vicar, it did and now he's done for. . . .
> Listen Marta. That's how it was with *that* love. "God is love, and love is God. Love is the proof of God's existence. Love exists as something real in the world of man and woman." I know the jargon, as you can hear. I've been an attentive listener to the vicar's outpourings . . .[18]

After the organist leaves her to go up to the choir loft Marta sits in the back of the church in a posture of prayer. She says in a desperate tone "If we could dare to show each other tenderness. If we could believe in a truth . . . If we could believe . . ."[19] Bergman cuts to the sacristy where the sacristan is telling Tomas that Marta is the only one in the church. Tomas decides to go out to say Vespers and the film ends as he turns to the congregation (Marta) and says "Holy, holy, holy, Lord God Almighty. All the earth is full of his glory . . ." Some communion has taken place between Marta and Tomas. Her "prayer" that they show one another some tenderness has been answered. Tomas' recitation of Vespers, whatever else it is, is a gesture toward her. In discussing the film, Bergman said:

> The man in *Winter Light*, the pastor, is nothing. He's nearly dead, you understand. He's almost completely cut off from everyone. The central character is the woman. She doesn't believe in God, but she has strength: it's the women who are strong. She can love. She can save with her love. Her problem is that she doesn't know how to express this love. She's ugly, clumsy. She smothers him, and he hates her for it and

for her ugliness. But she finally learns how to love. Only at the end, when they're in the empty church for the three o'clock service that has become perfectly meaningless for him, her prayer in a sense is answered: he responds to her love by going on with the service in that empty country church. It's his own first step toward feeling, toward learning how to love. We're saved not by God, but by love. That's the most we can hope for.[20]

In *The Silence* Bergman places two sisters, Anna and Ester, and Anna's young son Johan in the fictional foreign country of Timolka. They are journeying home. However, Ester is dying. Her condition is so bad that Anna eventually leaves her at the hotel to die as she continues to travel home with her son.

There is little love between Anna and Ester. Neither is successful about expressing her emotions. Ester, a translator by profession, is accused by Anna of being cold and unfeeling. Anna in her search for love and affection has become promiscuous. Her affection for her child seems more than tinged with eroticism. The child, Johan, seems largely confused throughout the film as he observes his mother and dying aunt. He is very much like the viewer of the film fascinated and curious about the two women. To suggest the loneliness and the lovelessness of the two women's lives, Bergman shoots the film in various dark shades with very little light or sunshine. As Johan curiously wanders through the dark corridors of the hotel, eventually becoming lost, he is not unlike a journeyman searching within the world for some insight or meaning that might enlighten the world's darkness.

In her hotel room Ester learns some words of the language that is spoken in Timolka. Two of the words she learns are the words for face and hand. When Anna and Johan are leaving to return home Ester realizes that she will die alone in the hotel. She gives Johan a secret message with words in a foreign language, the

Anna (Gunnel Lindblom), Johan (Jorgen Lindström) and Ester (Ingrid Thulin) on the train to Timolka, a city in which they will not understand the language.

words for hand and face. She tells him that the message is terribly important. When Anna and Johan are on the train traveling homeward Johan reads the message. He doesn't understand it completely, but there is some hint of a hope that perhaps he will incorporate into his own life the love that is so lacking in the life of his mother and aunt. Bergman has said "For me the important thing is that Ester sends a secret message to the boy. That's the important thing: the message he spells out to himself. To me Ester in all her misery represents a distillation of something indestructibly human, which the boy inherits from her."[21]

When Bergman's *The Touch* appeared some reviewers, perhaps guided by Bergman's description of the film as his first love story, wrote about *The Touch* as though Bergman had not explored the meaning of love previously.[22] Actually the film followed a long line of Bergman explorations into love. The title of the film tells it all. Before the credits appear on the screen Karin (magnificently played by Bibi Andersson) is rushing to the hospital. When she arrives there she is told that her mother has had a peaceful death. Bergman uses his camera especially cleverly in this scene: he intercuts between the dead woman's hand and objects in the room. A wedding ring is quite visible on the hand of the dead woman. Through these shots Bergman establishes the theme: the battle between "touch" (love) and death. The remainder of his film is a more detailed exploration of what Bergman has visually stated in the pre-credit sequence.

The story centers around a love triangle involving Karin and her husband Dr. Andreas Vergerus (Max von Sydow), and a Jewish London archeologist, David, who is doing excavation among religious ruins. Shortly after they meet Karin and David begin a love affair. The main metaphor that Bergman uses in the film is, of course, touch. No one seems to touch another successfully. Loving contact is never quite made. Toward the end of the film Karin learns through David's sister with whom he probably has an incestuous relationship that David has an arthritic condition in his hands. This suggests David's inability to touch anyone lovingly. There is one brief scene in which David and Karin seem to make contact temporarily. They are holding hands while standing outside the church in which David is doing his excavations. David says to Karin that they are really close to one another, that they are really meeting one another. In the scene it seems to be a sign of another age, an age more ordered and secure in which people could relate to one another lovingly. The closeness between David and Karin is eventually destroyed. The film ends with Karin, having decided to go back with her husband rather than with David, alone on a road. David has just walked away. The viewer has a strong sense that the drama has not really ended but that Bergman will pick up the theme in future films. And of course he did.

Bergman's *Scenes from a Marriage* appeared in this country in two forms: as a feature film and in the form in which it was originally made, as a six-part television series. Both forms were excellent works of art. Writing about the film which ran a little less than three hours Vincent Canby, the daily reviewer for *The New York Times*, wrote:

It's a movie of such extraordinary intimacy that it has the effect of breaking into mysterious components many things we ordinarily accept without thought, familiar and banal objects, faces, attitudes and emotions, especially love . . . In *Scenes from a Marriage* Mr. Bergman is examining the molecular structure of a human relationship. You think you've seen it before, but every time you see it, it's new, which is one of the things about love. Like a laboratory model of a molecule, the design is complex and beautiful in a purely abstract way, but the film is also intensely, almost unbearably moving.[23]

Canby is correct in pointing out that the film is almost unbearably moving. With the insight and skill of a genius, Bergman so dissects a marriage that some viewers find the film too painful to watch. Bergman does succeed in showing us familiar objects but under a new light: we see everything in the presence of Marianne (Liv Ullmann) and Johan (Erland Josephson) and we see everything stained by the pain and suffering that characterize their relationship. Through the film we feel as though we have come to know Marianne and Johan intimately.

The master of the closeup, Bergman uses this technique very effectively in *Scenes from a Marriage*. The effect of the closeup is to force a kind of claustrophobic effect on the viewer: there is no getting away from Marianne and Johan and their struggles to relate in love. Though other characters are in the story their presence and purpose are merely to call our attention to what's happening between Marianne and Johan. For example, in the first episode Marianne and Johan are having a dinner party for another couple (Bibi Andersson and Jan Malmsjö). The couple begin to pick on one another and gradually the viewer is being led into the middle of a hellish marriage. Marianne and Johan are shocked and embarrassed but the battle is just a foreshadowing of what will happen between the two of them who are supposedly in an ideal marriage. We discover later that the battling couple have been mirror-images of what Marianne and Johan become.

Later in the first segment which is entitled "Innocence and Panic" Marianne, with Johan's encouragement, has an abortion. The following is a summary of the other five segments: "The Art of Sweeping under the Rug"—Johan is disappointed at not advancing professionally and Marianne does not reach out to comfort him; "Paula"—Johan announces that he is leaving Marianne to be with a younger woman and Marianne is devastated by this, "The Vale of Tears"—after several years Johan, for whom things have not gone well, pays a visit to Marianne but they don't seem able to reconcile; "The Illiterates"—meeting to file divorce papers they lose control and lash out at one another physically; "In the Middle of the Night in a Dark House"—each has remarried but when they meet they seem to have reached a new understanding of themselves and one another. Of course the titles and summary barely hint at the cinematic richness and dramatic power of the film. The acting of Liv Ullmann and Erland Josephson is excellent. Their skill allows us to become sick of the characters they portray without causing us to dislike the work of art nor lose our admiration for the two performers.

The more that Marianne and Johan try to impose order on their lives the more disastrous the effects.[24] In the first episode Marianne and Johan are interviewed by a magazine writer. Johan is asked if he is afraid of the future and he responds:

If I stopped to think I'd be petrified with fear. Or so I imagine. So I don't think. I'm fond of this cozy old sofa and that oil lamp. They give me an illusion of security which is so fragile that it's almost comic. I like Bach's "St. Matthew Passion" though I'm not religious, because it gives me feelings of piety and belonging. Our families see a lot of each other and I depend very much on this contact, as it reminds me of my childhood when I felt I was protected. I like what Marianne said about fellow-feeling. It's good for a conscience which worries on quite the wrong occasions. I think you must have a kind of technique to be able to live and be content with your life. In fact, you have to practice quite hard not giving a damn about anything: The people I admire most are those who can take life as a joke. I can't. I have too little sense of humor for a feat like that.[25]

The key way that the couple tries to establish order is through talk.[26] The couple talk at one another endlessly but we discover that very little communication, especially loving communication is taking place. In the magazine interview Marianne is asked about the vision of love in 1 Corinthians 13. She says that what Paul presents is an impossible ideal useful only to be read at weddings and other solemn occasions. She says:

I think it's enough if you're kind to the person you're living with. Affection is also a good thing. Comradeship and tolerance and a sense of humor. Moderate ambitions for one another. If you supply those ingredients, then . . . love's not so important.[27]

The ending of the last episode ties together all six. Marianne and Johan finally have achieved a loving relationship. In bed together in a summer cottage Marianne wakes up in the middle of the night and tells Johan of a dream she just had. In the dream Marianne had no hands. She is slithering in soft sand and she can't get hold of Johan. Bergman is underlining the nightmare that Marianne's life has been because she has not been able to lovingly touch Johan. As they sit in bed Marianne wonders whether she can love anyone. Johan says:

I think I love you in my imperfect way. And I think you love me in your stormy, emotional way. In fact I think that you and I love one another. In an earthly and imperfect way.[28]

For Bergman love is earthly not heavenly.[29] It is the only salvation available to human persons.

Conclusion: *Philosophizing on Bergman*

BERGMAN STANDS alone among contemporary filmmakers. A truly extraordinary artist, Bergman has probed cinematically into the human mystery with enormous artistic success. No other author or director has produced as many exceptionally powerful films as the Swedish author/director. The philosophical vision that emerges from a study of the film dramas that Bergman made during the twenty-five year period from 1957 to 1982 is bleak but not without hope, however fragile the presence of hope may seem.

Though once God was at the center of his cinema, both Bergman's films and his comments on those films reveal that, from a dominating presence, God has become a memory which, though it can not be completely forgotten, is decidedly peripheral. The human journey is toward death. As God's presence dissolved the human person had to look elsewhere for some meaning in human existence, some hope to cling to in the face of death. Art offers hints of explanations but without God's animating presence and the superstructure of meaning that religion once provided for the artist, art's "answers" can never be adequate. The only hope we have, according to Bergman, is human love. There is no heavenly hope. To make loving contact with one other human being or perhaps with many others is the only salvation available to us. St. John of the Cross said that in the evening of our lives we will be judged on how we have loved.

Marianne (Liv Ullmann) and Johan (Erland Josephson) enjoying their love during a happy moment.

Within a totally secular setting Bergman echoes the sentiment. No God will judge us. If we try to evaluate our human existence the norm must be our success or failure in loving. In Bergman's world the presence of love, though it does not point to the existence of God nor to a life beyond the grave nor to the radical meaningfulness of reality, does enable us to work, to create and to try to find some happiness on our human journey. For Bergman that is the only hope we have.

Notes

INTRODUCTION

1. James Joyce, *The Portrait of the Artist as a Young Man* in *The Portable James Joyce* (New York: The Viking Press, Revised edition, 1966), p. 526.

2. Rollo May, *The Courage to Create* (New York: W. W. Norton & Company, June 1975), pp. 22–24.

3. Brigitta Steene, *Ingmar Bergman: A Guide to References and Resources* (Boston, Mass.: G.K. Hall & Co., 1987).

4. Richard Blake, "When, Out of the Past," *America*, March 21, 1987. Blake claims that Woody Allen will some day be recognized as America's greatest film maker without qualification. I think Blake may be right but Allen has some distance to go before equaling Bergman.

5. John Simon, *Ingmar Bergman Directs* (New York: Harcourt Brace Jovanovich Inc., 1972), p. 41.

6. Vernon Young, *Cinema Borealis: Ingmar Bergman and the Swedish Ethos* (New York: David Lewis, 1971), p. 283.

7. Ingmar Bergman, *The Magic Lantern*. Translated from Swedish by Joan Tate (New York: Viking, 1988).

8. In his provocative study *The Influence of Existentialism on Ingmar Bergman: An Analysis of the Theological Ideas Shaping a Filmmaker's Art* (Lewiston/Quenston: The Edwin Mellen Press, 1986) Charles B. Ketcham discovers a number of philosophical insights in relation to Bergman's work but his basic thrust is theological.

9. Josef Pieper, *Leisure the Basis of Culture*. Translated by Alexander Dru (New York: Pantheon Books Inc., 1952), pp. 48–49.

10. *Ibid.*, pp. 51–52.

11. *Ibid.*, p. 57.

169

12. Etienne Gilson, *The Unity of Philosophical Experience* (New York: Charles Scribner's Sons, 1937), p. 306.

13. Robert Bellah, Richard Madsen, William M. Sullivan, Ann Swidler, and Steven M. Tipton, *Habits of the Heart: Individualism and Commitment in American Life* (Berkeley: University of California Press, 1985).

14. Christopher Lash, *The Culture of Narcissism* (New York: Norton, 1978).

15. Young, *op. cit.*, p. 236.

16. For those interested in studying Bergman's career in the theatre I recommend Lise-Lone Marker's and Frederick J. Marker's *Ingmar Bergman: Four Decades in the Theater* (London: Cambridge University Press, 1982).

17. For a commentary that includes discussion of Bergman's earlier films I recommend Jorn Donner's *The Films of Ingmar Bergman from "Torment" to "All These Women"* formerly titled *The Personal Vision of Ingmar Bergman.* Translated by Holger Leanadbergh (New York: Dover Publications, Inc., 1972).

18. Frank Gado, *The Passion of Ingmar Bergman* (Durham: Duke University Press, 1986). Gado reports:

Suddenly, Bergman claims, he realized his cinematic finale should spring free of the morbidity that had seized his imagination since the mid-sixties. What evolved from this thought was a large "tapestry," originally planned to stretch over five hours in a version for Swedish television and about half that length in a print cut down for theatrical release. A celebration of life, it would re-create the world of Bergman's childhood—so distant from the "twilight world" of the twentieth century's latter decades which he blamed for the enfeeblement of art (p. 495). Though Bergman made *After the Rehearsal* for television after *Fanny and Alexander* he so wanted *Fanny and Alexander* and not *After the Rehearsal* to be considered his last film that he tried to prevent *After the Rehearsal* from being shown commercially (p. 507).

19. Philip Mosley, *Ingmar Bergman: The Cinema as Mistress* (London: Marion Boyars, 1981), p. 62. I basically agree with Mosley in excluding Bergman's *So Close to Life* and *The Devil's Eye* because they

are, compared to most of the films made after *The Seventh Seal*, minor films.

CHAPTER ONE

1. Robert O. Johann, *Building the Human* (New York: Herder and Herder, 1968), p. 11.

2. Kenneth Gallagher, *The Philosophy of Gabriel Marcel* (New York: Fordham University Press, 1962), pp. 30–40.

3. For an excellent discussion of the holy, confer Rudolf Otto's classic *The Idea of the Holy*, Second Edition, trans. by John W. Howey (New York: Oxford University Press, 1950).

4. Søren Kierkegaard, *Concluding Unscientific Postscript*, translated from the Danish by David F. Swenson, completed after his death and provided with Introduction and Notes by Walter Lowrie (Princeton: Princeton University Press, 1941), p. 51. William Luijpen, *Existential Phenomenology*, rev. ed. (Pittsburgh: Duquesne University Press, 1969), pp. 31–32. If Luijpen's interpretation of Kierkegaard is accurate in saying that the Swedish thinker's understanding of personal is excessively private, then my view differs from Kierkegaard's. I think that which is most deeply personal is also universal.

5. Bernard Lonergan, *The Subject* (Milwaukee: Marquette University Press, 1968), p. 1.

6. Michael Novak, *The Experience of Nothingness* (New York: Harper & Row, 1970), p. 27.

7. Rollo May, "Contributions to Existential Psychotherapy," in *Existence*, ed. Rollo May (New York: Simon and Schuster, 1958), pp. 59–60.

8. Lonergan, *Method in Theology* (New York: Herder and Herder, 1972), pp. 235–244.

9. W. J. Norris Clarke, "Analytic Philosophy and Language about God," in *Christian Philosophy and Religious Renewal*, G. McLean (ed.) (Washington, D.C.: Catholic University of America Press, 1966), pp. 307–308.

10. John F. Haught, *What Is God?* (New York: Paulist Press, 1986), p. 100.

11. James P. Mackey, *The Problems of Religious Faith* (Dublin: Helicon Limited, 1972). Discussing the implications of adopting an absurdist position Mackey wrote "In the case now in question, the case of refusal of an affirmative response to the invitation contained in one's very awareness of contingent being, one would have to honestly and consistently face an alternative view of the universe, somewhat after the model of Jean-Paul Sartre's. For Sartre, the contingency of being-in-itself:

> is what consciousness expresses in anthropomorphic terms by saying that being is superfluous (*de trop*)—that is, that consciousness absolutely cannot derive being from anything, either from another being, or from a possibility, or from a necessary law. Uncreated, without reason for being, without any connection with another being, being-in-itself is *de trop* for eternity.

The psychological reaction which contemplation of the being of man's empirical world produces in Sartre can only be Nausea (the title of his most metaphysical novel)—the reaction of one enveloped by matter so alien to oneself; matter which is without reason for its existence, without purpose, therefore, also, is alien to a rational creature—yet it surrounds him and will finally swallow him up. In the last analysis the difference here is not between responding to an invitation or not, it is the difference between seeing existence, life as invitation and seeing it as absurd, offensive to the human mind." (pp. 86-87)

12. John Macquarie, *Existentialism* (Baltimore, Maryland: Penguin Books, 1973), pp. 138–142.

13. Sartre, "Existentialism is a Humanism" in *Existentialism from Dostoevsky to Sartre,* edited with an introduction, prefaces and new translations by Walter Kaufmann (New York: Meridian Books, 1956), p. 245.

14. Sartre, *The Flies* in *No Exit and Three Other Plays* (New York: Vantage Books, 1946), pp. 122–123.

15. Haught, *op. cit.,* pp. 47–68.

16. Martin Buber, *I-Thou* (New York: Charles Scribner's Sons, 1970), trans. by Walter Kaufmann.

17. Luijpen, *op. cit.,* pp. 54–63.

18. *Ibid.,* pp. 54–56.

19. *Ibid.,* pp. 274–286.

20. William Barrett's *Death of the Soul: From Descartes to the Computer* (Garden City, New York: Anchor Press/Doubleday, 1986) is very good on tracing the loss of the self in modern and contemporary philosophy.

21. Fredrick D. Wilhelmsen, *The Metaphysics of Love* (New York 1962), p. 139.

22. Jacques Maritain, *Art and Scholasticism and the Frontiers of Poetry* trans. by Joseph W. Evans (New York: Charles Scribner's Sons, 1962); *Creative Intuition in Art and Poetry* (New York: Meridian Books, 1955).

23. Andre Bazin, *What Is Cinema?* (Berkeley: University of California Press, 1967).

24. Bergman, *Four Screenplays of Ingmar Bergman.* Translated by Lars Melmstrom and David Kushner (New York: Simon and Schuster, 1960), p. xv.

25. Stig Björkman, Torsten Manns and Jonas Sima, *Bergman as Bergman: Interviews with Ingmar Bergman.* Translated from the Swedish by Paul Britten Austin (New York: Simon and Schuster, 1973), p. 139–140.

26. Joyce, *op. cit.,* p. 481.

27. Arthur Gibson, *The Silence of God: Creative Response to the Films of Ingmar Bergman* (New York: Harper & Row, Publishers, 1969).

28. John Simon is excessively hard and I think unjust in his criticism of Gibson's book which Simon describes as "a fanatically narrow-minded, singularly ill-written book" (*op. cit.,* pp. 170-171).

CHAPTER TWO

1. Bruce F. Kawin, *Mindscreen: Bergman, Godard and First-Person Film* (New Jersey: Princeton University Press, 1978), p. 104.

2. Young, *op. cit.,* p. 3.

3. From frontispiece in Peter Cowie's *Ingmar Bergman: A Critical Biography* (New York: Charles Scribner's Sons, 1982).

4. *Face to Face: A Film by Ingmar Bergman* translated from the Swedish by Alan Blair (New York: Pantheon Books, 1976), p. v.

5. V. F. Perkins, *Film as Film: Understanding and Judging Movies* (Baltimore: Penguin Books, 1972). I think the following quotation from Perkins has special significance when applied to a master like Bergman:

When we enter the cinema we have to accept the implications of a controlled viewpoint. Since the camera has no brain, it has vision but not perception. It is the filmmaker's task to restore the selectivity of the cinematic eye. In this process he may control our perception so that *his* vision and emphases dominate our response to the created world (p. 124).

6. Steene, *op. cit.*, p. 9.

7. Björkman, *op. cit.*, p. 177.

8. Bergman, *Four Screenplays, op. cit.*, p. xxi. In the Introduction Bergman says: "Philosophically, there is a book which was a tremendous experience for me: Eiono Kaila's *Psychology of the Personality.* His thesis that man lives strictly according to his needs—negative and positive—was shattering to me, but terribly true. And I built on this ground."

9. Björkman, *op. cit.*, p. 190.

10. *Ibid.*, p. 177.

11. Roy Armes, *The Ambiguous Image: Narrative Style in Modern European Cinema* (Bloomington: Indiana University Press, 1976), p. 97.

12. Quoted in Steene, *op. cit.*, p. 1.

13. *Ibid.*, p. 2.

14. *Ibid.*, p. 6.

15. Bergman formed over the years what almost amounted to a repertory company—same actors, cameraman and technicians. Discussing his relationship with his actors Bergman said:

I sit quietly at home, make all my preparations in detail, plan the sets and draw them in detail, until I have it all in my head. But as soon as I get into the studio with the camera and the actors, it can happen in the course of the first run-through that a tone of voice, a gesture, or some independent expression on the part of one of the actors makes me change the whole thing. Even though nothing's been said explicitly between us, I feel it will be better that way. Such an awful lot of things go on between me and the actors, on a level which defies analysis.

Ingrid Thulin once said: "When you begin talking to me, I don't understand a thing of what you mean. But when you don't talk to me, then I understand exactly what you're saying."

That's how it often is between me and my actors. The fact is, I'm part of them, the complementary part. (Björkman, *op. cit.*, pp. 56–57)

Concerning his relationship with his cameraman, Sven Nykvist, Bergman has said "We've developed a private language, so to speak. We hardly need to say a word. Before the filming begins we go through the film very carefully, to see how we imagine the lighting, check the lighting conditions, and then solve all lighting problems together." (Björkman, *op. cit.*, p. 206)

16. Björkman, *op. cit*, p. 120. When asked whether he put Max von Sydow into certain roles because he, Bergman, felt allied to them, the director responded "The fact is, there's an enigmatic relationship between Max and myself. He has meant a tremendous amount to me."

17. Steene, *op. cit.*, p. 6.

18. I think of Liv Ullmann's roles in *Persona* and *Face to Face.*

19. Donner, *op. cit.*, p. 136.

20. Steene, *Ingmar Bergman* (New York: Twayne Publishers, Inc., 1968), pp. 62–63.

21. *The Jerome Biblical Commentary,* edited by Raymond E. Brown, SS., Joseph A. Fitzpatrick, S.J., Roland F. Murphy, O. Carm. (Englewood Cliffs, New Jersey: Prentice-Hall, Inc., 1968), p. 478.

22. Steene, *Ingmar Bergman, op. cit.*, p. 61.

23. Peter Cowie, quoted in Steene, *Ingmar Bergman, op. cit.*, p. 62.

24. Quoted in Steene, *Ingmar Bergman, op. cit.*, p. 62.

25. Bergman, *Four Screenplays, op. cit.*, pp. 125–126.

26. Peter Cowie, *Swedish Cinema* (New York: A. S. Barnes & Co., Inc., 1966), p. 142. Of Jof and Mia, Bergman has said "Naturally they're Joseph and Maria, it's as simple as that" (Björkman, *op. cit.*, p. 116).

27. Cowie, *Swedish Cinema, op. cit.*, p. 143.

28. Bergman, *Four Screenplays, op. cit.*, p. 137.

29. *Ibid.*, p. 138.

30. Steene, *Ingmar Bergman, op. cit.*, p. 65.

31. Cowie, *Swedish Cinema, op. cit.*, pp. 145–146.

32. Bergman, *Four Screenplays, op. cit.*, pp. 153–154.

33. Bergman, "The Snakeskin Speech" in *Persona and Shame: The Screenplays of Ingmar Bergman.* Translated by Keith Bradfield (New York: Marion Boyars, 1976), pp. 11–15. In future notes the speech will be referred to as "Snakeskin."

34. Bergman, *Four Screenplays, op. cit.*, pp. 109–110.

35. Paisley Livingston, *Ingmar Bergman and the Rituals of Art* (Ithaca: Cornell University Press, 1982), p. 47.

36. *Ibid.*

37. *Ibid.*, p. 59.

38. Bergman, *Four Screenplays, op. cit.*, p. 148.

39. *Ibid.*, pp. 111–112.

40. *Ibid.*, p. 113.

41. Steene, *Ingmar Bergman, op. cit.*, p. 65.

42. Bergman, *Four Screenplays, op. cit.*, p. 162.

43. *Ibid.*, p. 163.

CHAPTER THREE

1. Paul Schrader. *Transcendental Style in Film,* Ozu, Bresson, Dreyer (Berkeley, Los Angeles: University of California Press, 1972). I highly recommend Schrader's treatment of Bresson.

2. Björkman, *op. cit.*, p. 219.

3. *Ibid.*, p. 41.

4. *Ibid.*

5. Robin Wood, *Ingmar Bergman* (New York: Praeger, 1969), p. 104. I disagree with Stanley Kauffmann's assessment of Bergman's work in the film: "The hazard, which he has by no means escaped, is that his films have become essentially arenas of spiritual wrestling for the author through his characters, rather than disciplined artistic experiences whose prime purpose is emotional involvement of the audi-

ence. Even for the most serious viewer, the final result—in this new film (*Virgin Spring*) as in others—must be called a failure in relation to the totality of its existence as art work . . ." "The Virgin Spring" in *Ingmar Bergman: Essays in Criticism,* edited by Stuart M. Kaminsky with Joseph Hill (London: Oxford University Press, 1975), pp. 224–225.

6. Bergman, *Four Screenplays, op. cit.,* p. 210.
7. *Ibid.,* p. 204.
8. *Ibid.,* p. 294.
9. Bergman, *A Film Trilogy.* Translated from the Swedish by Paul Britten Austin (London: Calder and Boyors, 1967), pp. 58–59.
10. Björkman, *op. cit.,* p. 164.
11. Bergman, *A Film Trilogy, op. cit.,* p. 76.
12. *Ibid.,* p. 78.
13. *Ibid.,* p. 86.
14. *Ibid.,* p. 87.
15. *Ibid.*
16. Björkman, *op. cit.,* p. 195.
17. *Ibid.,* p. 191.
18. Ketcham, *op. cit.,* pp. 280–285.
19. Young, *op. cit.,*
20. Björkman, *op. cit.,* p. 164.
21. Ketcham, *op. cit.,* p. 282.
22. Bergman, *Autumn Sonata.* Translated from the Swedish by Alan Blair (New York: Pantheon Books, 1978), pp. 19–30.
23. Gado, *op. cit.,* p. 498. "The film's title, which elevates Alexander's two-years-younger sister Fanny to an importance unsupported by the story, serves as an autobiographical marker of the very close ties Bergman had with his sister Margareta; that Alexander is a self-portrait is patent from the film's first frame, showing him with his puppet theater. (The actor who plays the role, Bertil Guve, so resembles Ingmar as a boy that one has to surmise he was chosen for that reason.) Numerous details also point to his childhood. The marble statue that Alexander sees move, for example, refers to the statue of Venus in the Akerblom apartment that Bergman once imagined came to life; the prominence given to the laterna magica recalls young

Ingmar's fascination with that toy; the stuffed bear Alexander clutches in several scenes marks another appearance of Baloo, the teddy bear that Bergman had previously resurrected in *The City* and in *From the Life of the Marionettes.*"

24. Bergman, *Fanny and Alexander.* Translated from the Swedish by Alan Blair (New York: Pantheon Books, 1982), p. 184.

25. *Ibid.*, pp. 191–192.

26. *Ibid.*, p. 195.

27. *Ibid.*, p. 200.

28. Gado, *op. cit.*, pp. 503–504.

29. Bergman, *Fanny and Alexander, op. cit.*, p. 199.

30. Gado, *op. cit.*, pp. 504–505.

CHAPTER FOUR

1. I tried to show similarities between Sartre and Bergman in "Bergman's 'Shame' and Sartre's 'Stare'," *Catholic World,* September, 1969, pp. 247–250.

2. Nikolai Berdyaev, *The Destiny of Man,* translated by Natalie Duddington (New York: Harper & Row, 1960), p. 249.

3. Mosley, *op. cit.*, p. 162.

4. In his *Naming the Whirlwind* (New York, The Bobbs-Merrill Company, Inc., 1969), Langdon Gilkey makes the point that though the philosophical anthropology of the modern American intelligentsia is basically the same as European existentialism the former strikes a stance of optimism while the latter tends toward pessimism. "But let us note that the ultimate vision is the same: man is set within a universe with neither a transcendent source nor an inherent or ultimate order; his context is constituted exhaustively by blind nature or a meaningless void, not hostile, to be sure, but empty of purpose, indifferent, a faceless mystery" (p. 47). Gilkey might have been describing a Bergman film!

5. Björkman, *op. cit.*, p. 162.

6. *Ibid.*, p. 133.

7. *Ibid.*, p. 146.

8. *Ibid.*, p. 148.

9. Wood, *op. cit.*, p. 73.

10. *Ibid.*

11. "The film was based on my experiences during that trip to Uppsala. It was all as simple, concrete, and tangible as that. And I had no difficulty at all in carrying it through. That dream about the coffin is one I've had myself, a compulsive dream of mine. Not that I was lying in the coffin myself. I made that up. But the bit where the hearse comes along and bumps into a lamppost, and the coffin falls out and tips out the corpse. I had dreamed that many times" (Björkman, *op. cit.*, p. 146).

12. Gado, *op. cit.*, p. 213. My summary of the nightmare relies on Gado's summary.

13. Bergman's letter to his staff in *The New Yorker*, Oct. 21, 1972, p. 38.

14. Cf. Maritain, *Creative Intuition in Art and Poetry, op. cit.*, and Bergman's statements on creative intuition quoted in chapter one, pp. 29-30.

15. Lauder, "What Is Ingmar Bergman's Answer to Death?" *The New York Times*, Sunday, Feb. 11, 1973, p. 15.

16. Ronald Friedland, *The New York Times*, Sunday, May 27, 1973, p. 11.

17. Bergman was aware that he was going to make a different kind of film as he prepared to make *Cries and Whispers*. He wrote to his staff about the film "it will look different from our earlier works, and this script will also look different. We shall strain the medium's resources in a rather complicated way (Letter to staff, *op. cit.*, p. 38). A good article on the cinematography in *Cries and Whispers* is John Barrow's "How Do You Photograph a Cry or Whisper?", *The New York Times*, Sunday, January 14, 1973, p. 13. Praising Bergman and his cinematographer, Sven Nykvist, Barrow wrote:

Cinematography involves more than light, though; it involves decisions as to focal lengths of lenses, camera movement, what will be encompassed in the frame. Here too, Bergman and Nykvist have elevated the technique to a new high; they have made a film of which each and every frame could hang in an art gallery.

The most evident weapon in their arsenal in "Cries and Whispers" is the closeup, in which perhaps as much as a third of the film is shot . . .

And forcible they [*closeups*] are, though not by dint of numbers, but because Bergman uses his camera as a scalpel; he does not so much "film" his people in closeup, as he does confront them, staring at them searching for some chink in their impenetrable armor, asking for some sign, some clue, some gesture, that will explicate their viciousness, their tenderness, their insipidity.

18. "Today we can say that at last the director writes in film. The image—its plastic composition and the way it is set in time, because it is founded on a much higher degree of realism—has at its disposal more means of manipulating reality and of modifying it from within. The film-maker is no longer the competitor of the painter and the playwright, he is, at last, the equal of the novelist" (Andre Bazin, *op. cit.* pp. 39–40).

19. Letter to staff, *op. cit.*, p. 39.

20. Hollis Alpert's "Bergman's Study in Scarlet," in *World*, Dec. 5, 1972, p. 68.

21. Script of *Cries and Whispers*, *The New Yorker*, Oct. 21, 1972, pp. 55–56.

22. *Ibid.*, p. 56.

23. *Ibid.*, p. 74.

24. Lauder, "A Hint of Hope in Bergman's Odyssey", *The Christian Century*, Oct. 27, 1976, pp. 936–938.

25. Bergman, *Face to Face* (New York: Pantheon, 1976), pp. 98–99.

26. *Ibid.*, p. 100.

27. *Ibid.*, pp. 102–103.

28. Philip T. Hartung, *Commonweal*, Jan. 31, 1969, p. 563; *Catholic Film Newsletter*, Vol. 34, Jan. 30, 1969, no. 2, p. 5; Pauline Kael, "A Sign of Life," *The New Yorker*, Dec. 28, 1968, pp. 56–59.

29. Björkman, *op. cit.*, p. 229.

30. Wood, *op. cit.*, p. 176.

31. *The Catholic Film Newsletter*, *op. cit.*, p. 5.

32. For an interesting discussion of Sartre's view of love confer Luijpen's *Existential Phenomenology, op. cit.,* pp. 286–304.
33. Kael, *op. cit.,* p. 59.

CHAPTER FIVE

1. Simon, *op. cit.,* p. 18.
2. Livingstone, *op. cit.,* p. 20.
3. *Ibid.,* p. 17.
4. *Ibid.*
5. *Ibid.*
6. "Snakeskin," p. 11.
7. "Snakeskin," p. 13.
8. "Snakeskin," pp. 14–15.
9. Bergman, *Four Screenplays, op. cit.,* pp. xxi–xxii.
10. "Persisting tenuously in a state of ambivalence, art is caught between two irreconcilable imperatives. Insofar as the artist must draw upon the model of ritual in order to continue, he is bound to a lost tradition. Yet the very vitality of his work—its impact on the public, its meaning, the interest it arouses—depends on that tradition and is determined by the degree to which the artist manages to lend credence to the model. If the modern artist, laboring within the outline left by the dead serpent's remains, is to regain the poison for his work, he can do so only by somehow recapturing the efficacy of ritual. Yet the ritual model has been made untenable by the very movement of modernity, that is, by the historical desacralization of traditional forms. An aesthetic renewal based on originality and the headlong movement of the avant-garde distances itself rapidly from the model, literally devouring it from within. It would seem that if art is to be truly modern it must obey this double imperative: to spring from the sacred, yet always to betray the sacred. Thus the link to the cult is severed, but without being fully severed. Although the relation to the sacred has been radically transformed, this very relation continues to determine art— negatively" (Livingstone, *op. cit.,* pp. 144–145).

11. "Such is Bergman's formulation of the 'unsolvable' dilemma facing the artist, and each of his major films attempts to respond to this single problem. For Bergman, a sustained and complete recognition of the nature of the modern situation is essential, and must precede and orient any effort to discover alternatives. The contradiction, once it has become known to the artist, cannot be resolved at a higher level, or by passing, in the Hegelian manner, into another mode of expression where the artist's wounds are healed by the philosopher's dialectic. Nor can Bergman accept those 'resolutions' achieved through ignorance or forgetting—conveniences widely adopted today in commercial films, granting them a false and repugnant vitality" (*ibid.*, p. 145).

12. Young, *op. cit.*, p. 283.

13. Livingstone, *op. cit.*, p. 243.

14. *Ibid.*, p. 243.

15. *Ibid.*, pp. 19–20.

16. *Ibid*, p. 69.

17. *Ibid.*, p. 243.

18. Björkman, *op. cit.*, pp. 80–81.

19. *Ibid.*, p. 81.

20. *Ibid.*, p. 172.

21. Bergman, *Through a Glass Darkly*, *op. cit.*, pp. 45–46.

22. Cowie, *Swedish Cinema*, *op. cit.*, p. 156.

23. Livingstone, *op. cit.*, pp. 74ff. I am indebted to Livingstone's excellent treatment.

24. Bergman, *Four Screenplays*, *op. cit.*, p. 260.

25. *Ibid.*, p. 293.

26. Livingstone, *op. cit.*, pp. 75–76.

27. *Ibid.*, p. 107.

28. *Ibid.*, pp. 107–109.

29. Quoted in Livingstone, *op. cit.*, p. 234.

30. Livingstone, *op. cit.*, p. 221.

31. Bergman, *Autumn Sonata, op. cit.*, p. 63.

32. *Ibid.*, p. 18.

33. Livingstone, *op. cit.*, p. 148; Björkman, *op. cit.*, p. 237. Bergman said: "Though of course it is about the artist and society."

34. Livingstone, *op. cit.*, p. 153.
35. Quoted in Livingstone, *op. cit.*, p. 157.
36. Björkman, *op. cit.*, p. 240.
37. Livingstone, *op. cit.*, p. 157.
38. *Ibid.*, p. 159.
39. *Ibid.*, pp. 165–166.
40. Susan Sontag, *"Persona:* The Film in Depth" in Kaminsky, *op. cit.*, p. 255.
41. Björkman, *op. cit.*, pp. 198–199.
42. *Ibid.*, p. 199.
43. Simon, *op. cit.*, p. 215.
44. Sontag, *op. cit.*, p. 262.
45. I am greatly indebted to Marilyn Johns Blackwell's detailed and insightful study *Persona: The Transcendent Image* (Chicago: University of Illinois Press, 1986).
46. Blackwell, *op. cit.*, p. 12.
47. *Ibid.*, pp. 12–13.
48. *Ibid.*, pp. 15–16.
49. "This shot also prefigures three images later in the film: one when Elisabeth's eyes pop open after Alma visits her at night, the second when we get a drastically foreshortened upside-down view of Alma as she thrashes about on her bed in insomnia, and the third when Elisabeth's upside-down face appears in the camera's viewfinder in the reflexive ending of the film. This unusual camera angle serves to shock us out of our customary expectations of visual representation, in effect turning our visual field on its head and disorienting us" *Ibid,* p. 26.
50. *Ibid.*, p. 29.
51. *Ibid.*, pp. 36–37.
52. Simon, *op. cit.*, p. 292.
53. Bergman, *Persona and Shame, op. cit.*, pp. 29–31.
54. *Ibid.*, pp. 41–42.
55. Kawin, *op. cit.*, p. 120.
56. Bergman, *Persona and Shame, op. cit.*, p. 47.
57. Blackwell, *op. cit.*, p. 69.
58. Bergman, *Persona and Shame, op. cit.*, p. 59.

59. Björkman, *op. cit.*, quoted on p. 75 of Blackwell who indicates she does not understand why the interview is not translated.

60. Simon, *op. cit.*, p. 292.

61. Bergman, *Persona and Shame, op. cit.*, p. 78.

62. Blackwell, *op. cit.*, p. 91.

63. Wood, *op. cit.*, p. 152.

64. Bergman, *Persona and Shame, op. cit.*, p. 81. The quote in the text is from the film itself and varies slightly from the script.

65. Blackwell, *op. cit.*, pp. 97–98.

66. Bergman, *Persona and Shame, op. cit.*, p. 97. The quote in the text is from the film itself and varies slightly from the script.

CHAPTER SIX

1. Bergman, *Four Screenplays, op. cit.*, p. 139.

2. Wood, *op. cit.*, pp. 73–74.

3. Bergman, *Four Screenplays, op. cit.*, pp. 179–180.

4. *Ibid.*, p. 180.

5. Obviously because I think the love between Anna and Agnes is genuine and beautiful I disagree with critic Joan Mellen who wrote of Anna: "She is the character most capable of loyalty and love in the film, yet her love amounts only to the animal consolation of physical nearness—all, Bergman says, of which woman is capable" (Kaminsky, *op. cit.*, p. 303).

6. *Ibid.*, pp. 293–312, *Catholic Film Newsletter,* January 15, 1973, Vol. 38, No. 1, p. 1.

7. Bergman, *Face to Face, op. cit.*, p. 105.

8. *Ibid.*, pp. 105–106.

9. *Ibid.*, p. 108.

10. Björkman, *op. cit.*, p. 235.

11. For an excellent analysis of the trilogy and some other Bergman films from a religious angle of vision, see Arthur Gibson, *The Silence of God, op. cit.*

12. "Playboy Interview: Ingmar Bergman," *Playboy Magazine*, June, 1964, p. 68.

13. Bergman, *A Film Trilogy, op. cit.*, p. 35.

14. *Ibid.*, p. 45.

15. *Ibid.*, pp. 45–46.

16. Björkman, *op. cit.*, pp. 166–168.

17. Bergman, *A Film Trilogy, op. cit.*, pp. 81–82.

18. *Ibid.*, pp. 102–103.

19. *Ibid.*, p. 104.

20. *Playboy, op. cit.*, p. 68.

21. Björkman, *op. cit.*, p. 183.

22. I commented on this in an article about *The Touch:* "Bergman's Odyssey," *America*, Sept. 4, 1971. In his review in *The New York Times* (July 15, 1971, p. 22) Vincent Canby wrote:

"Ingmar Bergman describes 'The Touch' as his first love story, which just goes to prove that a director, even one of the best, may often be a most unreliable source of information about his own work. If they aren't love stories, what in the name of God (who, in Bergman's world, is synonymous with enigmatic love)—are 'Shame' and 'The Passion of Anna'? What is 'The Hour of the Wolf'? In each of these films Bergman deals with aspects of love—with the cruelties of love, with the terrible absence of love, and with the processes by which love, in its own time, can die."

23. Canby, *New York Times*, September 16, 1974, p. 41.

24. In *America*, March 5, 1977, p. 203, Richard Blake is insightful on this point: "The self—Bergman, modern man, the viewer—wants desperately to control his life. He constructs a facade of respectability and order, but lives in terror that the wall will not hold. Powers beyond man's control threaten and inevitably overwhelm him. He may struggle heroically, like Camus's Sisyphus, but, in the end, the best he can hope for is the ability to cope. That is why there are so few happy endings in Bergman's films. Social injustice, his earliest concern, God, the love of man and woman, violence and art, his later concerns, all fit into a pattern. They refuse to submit to his drive for order. His happiest

characters are those who accept the madness of faith, or love, with no pretense of holding on to the appearances of rationality. But his major heroes, images of Bergman himself, are tormented by the world they cannot control and the realization that their facade of self-control and order is being stripped away from them."

25. Bergman, *Scenes from a Marriage* translated from the Swedish by Alan Blair in *The Marriage Scenarios* (New York: Pantheon Books, 1974), p. 13.

26. Janet Karsten Larson, "Schemes from a Marriage," *Christian Century*, June 1, 1977, p. 537.

27. Bergman, *Scenes from a Marriage, op. cit.*, p. 16.

28. *Ibid.*, p. 200.

29. Larson, *op. cit.*, p. 540, adds the following postscript to Bergman's exploration of marriage: "As it is, at the end one can only wonder what will become of Marianne's complacent soul without the influence of Johan's *angst*, his incessant questioning of their routine and the chaos beneath it. And what will become of his ailing soul without Marianne's instinct for health? Marriage is a scheme for bringing together these spiritual illiterates who need each other with their very earthly and imperfect love. In many of its forms it is not a scheme that works very smoothly in these times, but one cannot help hoping that somewhere in the world, Bergman's matched sufferers can find a breathing space to try again, in a seventh scene from their remarriage. And one must imagine them happy."

Selected Filmography

THE SEVENTH SEAL (*Det sjunde inseglet*)

Script: Ingmar Bergman. *Photography:* Gunnar Fischer. *Music:* Erik Nordgren. *Art Direction:* P.A. Lundgren. *Editing:* Lennart Wallén. *Choreography:* Else Fisher. *Costumes:* Manne Lindholm. *Makeup:* Carl M. Lundh (Nils Nittel). *Production Manager:* Allan Ekelund. *Production Company:* Svensk Filmindustri. 95 minutes. Swedish premiere: February 16, 1957.

Cast: Max von Sydow (the Knight, Antonius Block), Gunnar Björnstrand (Squire Jöns), Bengt Ekerot (Death), Nils Poppe (Jof), Bibi Andersson (Mia), Åke Fridell (Plog, the blacksmith), Inga Gill (Lisa, Plog's wife), Maud Hansson (witch), Inga Landgré (Knight's wife), Gunnel Lindblom (girl), Bertil Anderberg (Raval), Anders Ek (Monk), Gunnar Olsson (Albertus, the painter), Erik Strandmark (Skat), Benkt-Åke Benktsson (tavern owner), Ulf Johansson (leader of the soldiers), Lars Lind (young monk), Gudrun Brost (woman in tavern), Ove Svensson (corpse on hillside).

WILD STRAWBERRIES (*Smultronstället*)

Script: Ingmar Bergman. *Photography:* Gunnar Fischer. *Music:* Erik Nordgren. *Art Direction:* Gittan Gustafsson. *Editing:* Oscar Rosander. *Costumes:* Millie Ström. *Makeup:* Carl M. Lundh (Nils Nittel). *Production Manager:* Allan Ekelund. *Production Company:* Svensk Filmindustri. 90 minutes. Swedish premiere: December 26, 1957.

GOD, DEATH, ART AND LOVE

Cast: Victor Sjöström (Professor Isak Borg), Bibi Andersson (Sara),
Ingrid Thulin (Marianne), Gunnar Björnstrand (Evald), Folke
Sundquist (Anders), Björn Bjelvenstam (Viktor), Nalma
Wifstrand (Isak's mother), Jullan Kindahl (Agda, the
housekeeper), Gunnar Sjöberg (Alman), Gunnel Broström (Mrs.
Alman), Gertrud Fridh (Isak's wife), Åke Fridell (her lover), Max
von Sydow (Åkerman), Sif Ruud (aunt), Yngve Nordwall (Uncle
Aron), Per Sjöstrand (Sigfrid), Gio Petré (Sigbritt), Gunnel
Lindblom (Charlotta), Maud Hansson (Angelica), Anne-Marie
Wiman (Mrs. Åkerman), Eva Norée (Anna), Lena Bergman,
Monica Ehrling (twins), Per Skogsberg (Hagbart), Göran
Lundquist (Benjamin), Prof. Sigge Wulff (rector, Lund
University).

THE MAGICIAN (*Ansiktet*)

Script: Ingmar Bergman. *Photography:* Gunnar Fischer. *Music:* Erik
Nordgren. *Art Direction:* P.A. Lundgren. *Editing:* Oscar Rosander.
Costumes: Manne Lindholm, Greta Johansson. Makeup: Börje
Lundh, Nils Nittel. *Production Manager:* Allan Ekelund. *Production
Company:* Svensk Filmindustri. 100 minutes. Swedish premiere:
December 26, 1958.

Cast: Max von Sydow (Albert Emanuel Vogler), Ingrid Thulin
(Manda Vogler), Åke Fridell (Tubal), Naima Wifstrand (Vogler's
grandmother), Gunnar Björnstrand (Dr. Anders Vergérus), Bengt
Ekerot (Spegel), Bibi Andersson (Sara Lindqvist), Gertrud Fridh
(Ottilia Egerman), Erland Josephson (Consul Abraham Egerman),
Lars Ekborg (Simson, the coachman), Toivo Pawlo (Frans
Starbeck), Ulla Sjöblom (Mrs. Starbeck), Axel Düberg (Rustan,
the butler), Birgitta Pettersson (Sanna, the maid), Oscar Ljung
(Antonsson), Sif Ruud (Sofia Garp).

THE VIRGIN SPRING (*Jungfrukällan*)
Script: Ulla Isaksson, based on a fourteenth-century legend, "Töres dotter i Wänge." *Photography:* Sven Nykvist. *Music:* Erik Nordgren. *Art Direction:* P.A. Lundgren. *Production Buyer:* Karl-Arne Bergman. *Editing:* Oscar Rosander. *Costumes:* Marik Vos. *Makeup:* Börje Lundh. *Production Manager:* Allan Ekelund. *Production Company:* Svensk Filmindustri. 88 minutes. Swedish premiere: February 8, 1960
Cast: Max von Sydow (Töre), Birgitta Valberg (Märeta), Birgitta Pettersson (Karin), Gunnel Lindblom (Ingeri), Axel Düberg (thin herdsman), Tor Isedal (mute herdsman), Allan Edwall (beggar), Ove Porath (boy), Axel Slangus (Odin worshipper), Gudrun Brost (Frida), Oscar Ljung (Simon), Tor Borong, Leif Forstenberg (farm hands).

THROUGH A GLASS DARKLY (*Såsom i en spegel*)
Script: Ingmar Bergman. *Photography:* Sven Nykvist. *Music:* Erik Nordgren, with extracts from Bach, played by Erling Blöndal Bengtsson. *Art Direction:* P.A. Lundgren. *Editing:* Ulla Ryghe. *Production Buyer:* Karl-Arne Bergman. *Costumes:* Mago. *Production Manager:* Allan Ekelund. *Production Company:* Svensk Filmindustri. 89 minutes. Swedish premiere: October 16, 1961
Cast: Harriet Andersson (Karin), Gunnar Björnstrand (David, her father), Max von Sydow (Martin, Karin's husband), Lars Passgård (Fredrik, David's son, known as Minus).

WINTER LIGHT (*Nattvardsgästerna*)
Script: Ingmar Bergman. *Photography:* Sven Nykvist. *Music:* from *The Swedish Hymnal. Art Direction:* P.A. Lundgren. *Production Buyer:* Karl-Arne Bergman. *Editing:* Ulla Ryghe. *Costumes:* Mago. *Makeup:* Börje Lundh. *Production Manager:* Allan Ekelund.

Production Company: Svensk Filmindustri. 80 minutes. Swedish premiere: February 11, 1963
Cast: Ingrid Thulin (Märta Lundberg), Gunnar Björnstrand (Thomas Eriksson), Gunnel Lindblom (Karin Persson), Max von Sydow (Jonas Persson), Allan Edwall (Algot Frövik), Kolbjörn Knudsen (Knut Aronsson), Olof Thunberg (Fredrik Blom, organist), Elsa Ebbesen-Thornblad (Magdalena Ledfors), Tor Borong (Johan Åkerblom), Bertha Sånnell (Hanna Appelblad), Helena Palmgren (Doris), Eddie Axberg (Johan Strand), Lars-Owe Carlberg (local police officer).

THE SILENCE (*Tystnaden*)
Script: Ingmar Bergman. *Photography:* Sven Nykvist. *Music:* Ivan Renliden, R. Mersey, J.S. Bach (*Goldberg Variations*). *Art Direction:* P.A. Lundgren. *Production Buyer:* Karl-Arne Bergman. *Editing:* Ulla Ryghe. *Costumes:* Marik Vos-Lundh, Bertha Sånnell. *Makeup:* Gullan Westfelt. *Production Manager:* Allan Ekelund. *Production Company:* Svensk Filmindustri. 95 minutes. Swedish premiere: September 23, 1963.

Cast: Ingrid Thulin (Ester), Gunnel Lindblom (Anna), Jörgen Lindström (Johan, her son), Håkan Jahnberg (old waiter), Birger Malmsten (waiter in bar), the Eduardinis (seven dwarfs), Eduardo Gutierrez (the dwarfs' manager), Lissi Alandh and Leif Forstenberg (couple in the theater), Karl-Arne Bergman (newsboy), Olof Widgren (old man in hotel corridor), Kristina Olansson (stand-in for Gunnel Lindblom in sex scene).

PERSONA
Script: Ingmar Bergman. *Photography:* Sven Nykvist. *Music:* Lars Johan Werle, with extract from Bach. *Art Direction:* Bibi Lindström. *Production Buyer:* Karl-Arne Bergman. *Editing:* Ulla Ryghe. Costumes: Mago. *Makeup:* Börje Lundh, Tina Johansson.

Sound Effects: Evald Andersson. *Production Manager:* Lars-Owe Carlberg. *Production Company:* Svensk Filmindustri. 84 minutes. Swedish premiere: October 18, 1966.

Cast: Bibi Andersson (Nurse Alman), Liv Ullmann (Elisabet Vogler), Margaretha Krook (psychiatrist), Gunnar Björnstrand (Mr. Vogler), Jörgen Lindström (Elisabet's son).

HOUR OF THE WOLF (*Vargtimmen*)

Script: Ingmar Bergman. *Photography:* Sven Nykvist. *Music:* Lars Johan Werle, with extracts from Mozart and Bach. *Art Direction:* Marik Vos-Lundh. *Production Buyer:* Karl-Arne Bergman. *Editing:* Ulla Ryghe. *Costumes:* Mago, Eivor Kullberg. *Makeup:* Börje Lundh, Kjell Gustavsson, Tina Johansson. *Production Manager:* Lars-Owe Carlberg. *Production Company:* Svensk Filmindustri. 89 minutes. Swedish premiere: February 19, 1968.

Cast: Max von Sydow (Johan Borg), Liv Ullmann (Alma Borg, his wife), Ingrid Thulin (Veronica Vogler), Georg Rydeberg (Archivist Lindhorst), Erland Josephson (Baron von Merkens), Gertrud Fridh (Corinne von Merkens), Naima Wifstrand (demon who removes her face), Bertil Anderberg (Ernst von Merkens), Ulf Johansson (Curator Heerbrand), Lenn Hjortzberg (Kapellmeister Kreisler), Agda Helin (maid at Merkens castle), Mikael Rundquist (boy in jeans), Folke Sundquist (Tamino in puppet theater). Cut: Mona Seilitz (corpse in mortuary).

SHAME (*Skammen*)

Script: Ingmar Bergman. *Photography:* Sven Nykvist. *Art Direction:* P.A. Lundgren. *Production Buyer:* Karl-Arne Bergman. *Editing:* Ulla Ryghe. *Costumes:* Mago. *Production Manager:* Lars-Owe Carlberg. *Production Company:* Svensk Filmindustri/ Cinematograph. 102 minutes. Swedish premiere: September 29, 1968.

Cast: Liv Ullmann (Eva Rosenberg), Max von Sydow (Jan Rosenberg), Gunnar Björnstrand (Jacobi), Birgitta Valberg (Mrs. Jacobi), Sigge Fürst (Filip), Hans Alfredson (Lobelius), Ingvar Kjellson (Oswald), Frank Sundström (interrogator), Ulf Johansson (doctor), Frej Lindqvist (stooped man), Rune Lndström (stout gentleman), Willy Peters (older officer) Bengt Eklund (orderly), Åke Jörnfalk (condemned man), Vilgot Sjöman (interviewer), Lars Amble (an officer), Björn Thambert (Johan), Barbro Hiort af Ornäs (Mrs. Jacobi), Karl-Axel Forsberg (secretary), Gösta Přuzelius (pastor), Brita Oberg (woman in interrogation room), Agda Helin (woman in shop), Ellika Mann (prison warden), Monica Lindberg, Gregor Dahlman, Nils Whiten, Per Berglund, Stig Lindberg, Jan Bergman, Nils Fogeby, Brian Wikström, Georg Skarstedt, Lilian Carlsson, Börje Lundh, Eivor Kullberg, Karl-Arne Bergman.

THE RITE (*Riten*)

Script: Ingmar Bergman. *Photography:* Sven Nykvist. *Art Direction;* Lennart Blomkvist. *Editing:* Siv Kanälv. *Costumes:* Mago. *Production Manager:* Lars-Owe Carlberg. *Production Company:* Svensk Filmindustri/Sveriges TV/Cinematograph. 74 minutes. Swedish premiere (on Swedish television) March 25, 1969.

Cast: Ingrid Thulin (Thea Winkelmann), Anders Ek (Albert Emmanuel Sebastian Fischer), Gunnar Björnstrand (Hans Winkelmann), Erik Hell (Judge Abramsson), Ingmar Bergman (priest in confessional).

THE PASSION OF ANNA (*En passion*)

Script: Ingmar Bergman. *Photography* (Eastmancolor): Sven Nykvist. *Music:* extracts from Bach, and Allan Gray's song, "Always Romantic." *Art Direction:* P.A. Lundgren. *Production Buyer:* Karl-

Arne Bergman. *Editing:* Siv Kanälv. *Costumes:* Mago. *Hairstyles:*
Börje Lundh. *Production Manager:* Lars-Owe Carlberg. *Production
Company:* Svensk Filmindustri/Cinematograph. 101 minutes.
Swedish premiere: November 10, 1969.

Cast: Liv Ullman (Anna Fromm), Bibi Andersson (Eva Vergérus),
Max von Sydow (Andreas Winkelmann), Erland Josephson (Elis
Vergérus), Erik Hell (Johan Andersson), Sigge Fürst (Verner),
Svea Holst (Verner's wife), Annika Kronberg (Katarina), Hjördis
Pettersson (Johan's sister), Lars-Owe Carlberg, Brian Wikström
(policemen), Barbro Hiort af Ornäs, Malin Ek, Britta Brunius,
Brita Oberg, Marianne Karlbeck, Lennart Blomkvist.

THE TOUCH (*Beröringen*)

Script: Ingmar Bergman. *Photography* (Eastmancolor): Sven Nykvist.
Music: Jan Johansson. *Art Direction:* P.A. Lundgren. *Editing:* Siv
Kanälv-Lundgren. *Title Sequence Photography:* Gunnar Fischer.
Production Manager: Lars-Owe Carlberg. *Production Company:*
ABC Pictures (New York)/Cinematograph (Stockholm). 113
minutes. Swedish premiere: August 30, 1971.

Cast: Elliott Gould (David Kovac), Bibi Andersson (Karin Vergérus),
Max von Sydow (Dr. Andreas Vergérus), Sheila Reid (Sara
Kovac), Barbro Hiort af Ornäs (Karin's mother), Staffan
Hallerstam (Anders Vergérus), Maria Nolgård (Agnes Vergérus),
Åke Lindstrom (doctor), Mimmi Wahlander (nurse), Else
Ebbesen (matron), Anna von Rosen, Karin Nilsson (neighbors),
Erik Nyhlen (archeologist), Margareta Byström (Dr. Vergérus's
secretary), Alan Simon (museum curator), Per Sjöstrand (another
curator), Aino Taube (woman on staircase), Ann-Christin
Lobraten (museum worker), Dennis Gotobed (British
immigration officer), Bengt Ottekil (London bellboy), Harry
Schein, Stig Björkman (guests at party).

CRIES AND WHISPERS (*Viskningar och rop*)

Script: Ingmar Bergman. *Photography* (Eastmancolor): Sven Nykvist. *Music:* Chopin, played by Käbi Laretei: Bach, played by Pierre Fournier. *Art Direction:* Marik Vos. *Editing:* Siv Lundgren. *Production Manager:* Lars-Owe Carlberg. *Production Company:* Cinematograph, in association with Svenska Filminstitutet. 91 minutes. Swedish premiere: March 5, 1973.

Cast: Harriet Andersson (Agnes), Kari Sylwan (Anna), Ingrid Thulin (Karin), Liv Ullmann (Maria), Erland Josephson (David, Maria's lover), Henning Moritzen (Joakim), George Åhlin (Fredrik), Anders Ek (Pastor Isak), Inga Gill (Aunt Olga), Malin Gjörup, Rosanna Mariano, Lena Bergman, Monika Priede, Greta Johanson, Karin Johanson.

SCENES FROM A MARRIAGE (*Scener ur ett äktenskap*)

Script: Ingmar Bergman. *Photography* (Eastmancolor 16 mm): Sven Nykvist. *Art Direction:* Björn Thulin. *Editing:* Siv Lundgren. *Production Manager:* Lars-Owe Carlberg. *Production Company:* Cinematograph. 168 minutes (theatrical version). Swedish premiere (on television, in six weekly parts): April 11 through May 16, 1973.

Cast: Liv Ullmann (Marianne), Erland Josephson (Johan), Bibi Andersson (Katarina), Jan Malmsjö (Peter), Anita Wall (interviewer), Gunnel Lindblom (Eva), Barbro Hiort af Ornäs (Mrs. Jacobi), Bertil Norström, Arne Carlsson. (Wenche Foss plays Marianne's mother in the TV version.)

FACE TO FACE (*Ansikte mot Ansikte*)

Script: Ingmar Bergman. *Photography* (Eastmancolor): Sven Nykvist. *Music:* Mozart, played by Käbi Laretei. *Art Direction:* Anne Terselius-Hagegård, Anna Asp, Maggie Strindberg. *Set*

Decoration: Peter Krupenin. *Editing:* Siv Lundgren. *Producers:* Ingmar Bergman, Lars-Owe Carlberg. *Production Manager:* Katinka Faragó. *Production Company:* Cinematograph. 136 minutes. Swedish premiere (on television, in four weekly parts): April 28 through May 19, 1976.

Cast: Liv Ullmann (Dr. Jenny Isaksson), Erland Josephson (Dr. Thomas Jacobi), Gunnar Björnstrand (grandfather), Aino Taube (grandmother), Kari Sylwan (Maria), Sif Ruud (Elisabeth Wankel), Sven Lindberg (Dr. Erik Isaksson), Tore Segelcke (lady), Ulf Johanson (Dr. Helmuth Wankel), Helen Friberg (Anna), Kristina Adolphson (Veronica), Gösta Ekman (Mikael Strömberg), Käbi Laretei (concert pianist), Birger Malmsten (rapist), Göran Stangertz (second rapist), Marianne Aminoff (Jenny's mother), Gösta Prüzelius (clergyman), Rebecca Pawlo, Lena Ohlin (boutique girls).

THE SERPENT'S EGG (*Das Schlangenei*) (Swedish Title *Ormens ägg*)

Script: Ingmar Bergman. *Photography* (Eastmancolor): Sven Nykvist. *Additional Photography:* Peter Rohe, Dieter Lohmann. *Music:* Rolf Wilhelm. *Production Designer:* Rolf Zehetbauer. *Art Direction:* Erner Achmann, Herbert Strabel. *Editing:* Jutta Hering, Petra von Oelffen. *Choreography:* Heino Hallhuber. *Costumes:* Charlotte Fleming. *Producer:* Dino De Laurentiis. *Executive Producer:* Horst Wendlandt. *Production Manager:* Georg Föcking. *Production Executive:* Harold Nebenzal. *Production Company:* Rialto Film (West Berlin)/Dino De Laurentiis Corporation (Los Angeles). 119 minutes. Filmed in English. German premiere: October 26, 1977.

Cast: Liv Ullmann (Manuela Rosenberg), David Carradine (Abel Rosenberg), Gert Froebe (Inspector Bauer), Heinz Bennent (Hans Vergérus), James Whitmore (priest), Glynn Turman

(Monroe), Georg Hartmann (Hollinger), Edith Heerdegen (Mrs. Holle), Kyra Mladeck (Miss Dorst), Fritz Strassner (Dr. Soltermann), Hans Quest (Dr. Silbermann), Wolfgang Weiser (civil servant), Paula Braend (Mrs. Hemse), Walter Schmidinger (Solomon), Lisi Mangold (Mikaela), Grischa Huber (Stella), Paul Bürks (cabaret comedian), Toni Berger (Mr. Rosenberg), Erna Brunell (Mrs. Rosenberg), Hans Eichler (Max Rosenberg).

AUTUMN SONATA (*Herbstsonat*) (Swedish Title: *Höstsonaten*)
Script: Ingmar Bergman. *Photography* (Eastmancolor): Sven Nykvist. *Music:* Chopin, played by Käbi Laretei; Bach, performed by Claude Genetay; and Handel, performed by Frans Brüggen, Gustav Leonhardt, and Anne Bylsma. *Set Design:* Anna Asp. *Editing:* Sylvia Ingemarsson. *Costumes:* Inger Pehrsson. *Production Supervisors:* Ingrid Karlebo Bergman, Lars-Owe Carlberg. *Production Manager:* Katinka Faragó. *Production Company:* Personafilm for ITC. 92 minutes. Swedish Premiere: October 8, 1978.

Cast: Ingrid Bergman (Charlotte), Liv Ullmann (Eva), Lena Nyman (Helena), Halvar Björk (Viktor), Arne Bang-Hansen (Uncle Otto), Gunnar Björnstrand (Paul), Erland Josephson (Josef), Georg Lokkeberg (Leonardo), Linn Ullmann (Eva as a child), Knut Wigert (professor), Eva von Hanno (nurse), Marianne Aminoff, Mimi Pollak.

FROM THE LIFE OF THE MARIONETTES (*Aus dem Leben der Marionetten*)
Script: Ingmar Bergman. *Photography* (part Eastmancolor): Sven Nykvist. *Music:* Rolf Wilhelm. Song, "Touch Me, Take Me" (in English, singer uncredited). *Production Design:* Rolf Zehetbauer. *Art Direction:* Herbert Strabel. *Set Decoration:* Rolf Zehetbauer. *Editing:* Petra von Oelffen (English-language version: Geri

Ashur). *Costumes:* Charlotte Flemming, Egon Strasser. *Makeup:* Mathilde Basedow. *Production Manager:* Paulette Hufnagel, Irmgard Kelpinski. *Producers:* Horst Wendlandt, Ingrid Karlebo Bergman, Richard Brick (English-language version). *Production Company:* Personafilm (Munich), in collaboration with Bayerische Staatsschauspiel. 104 minutes. Premiere: 1980.

Cast: Robert Atzorn (Peter Egermann), Martin Benrath (Professor Mogens Jensen), Christine Buchegger (Katarina Egermann), Rita Russek (Katarina Krafft, known as Ka), Lola Müthel (Cordelia Egermann), Walter Schmidinger (Thomas Isidor Mandelbaum, known as Tim), Heinz Bennent (Arthur Brenner), Ruth Olafs (nurse), Karl-Heinz Pelser (police investigator), Gaby Dohm (Peter Egermann's secretary), Toni Berger (brothel doorman), Erwin Faber, Doris Jensen.

FANNY AND ALEXANDER (*Fanny och Alexander*)
Script: Ingmar Bergman. *Photography* (Eastmancolor): Sven Nykvist. *Music:* Daniel Bell. *Art Direction:* Anna Asp. *Set Decoration:* Kaj Larsen. *Editing:* Sylvia Ingemarsson. *Wardrobe:* Marik Vos-Lundh. *Makeup:* Leif Qviström, Anna-Lena Melin, Barbro Holmberg-Haugen. *Production Manager:* Katinka Faragó. *Administration:* Lars-Owe Carlberg, Ingrid Karlebo Bergman, Fredrik von Rosen, Hellen Igler. *Executive Producer:* Jörn Donner. *Production Company:* Svenska Filminstitutet (Stockholm)/Sveriges TV 1 (Stockholm)/Personafilm (Munich)/Gaumont (Paris). 199 minutes (first version in theatrical release). Swedish Premiere: Christmas, 1982.

Cast: Gunn Wållgren (Helena Ekdahl), Allan Edwall (Oscar Ekdahl), Ewa Fröling (Emilie Ekdahl), Bertil Guve (Alexander), Pernilla Allwin (Fanny), Börje Ahlstedt (Carl Ekdahl), Christina Schollin (Lydia Ekdahl), Jarl Kulle (Gustav Adolf Ekdahl), Mona Malm (Alma Ekdahl), Maria Granlund (Petra), Emelie Werkö

(Jenny), Kristian Almgren (Putte), Angelica Wallgren (Eva),
Majlis Granlund (Miss Vega), Svea Holst-Widén (Miss Ester),
Siv Ericks (Alida), Inga Ålenius (Lisen), Kristina Adolphson
(Siri), Evan von Hanno (Berta), Pernilla Wallgren (Maj), Käbi
Laretei (Aunt Anna), Sonya Hedenbratt (Aunt Emma), Erland
Josephson (Isak Jacobi), Mats Bergman (Aron), Stina Ekblad
(Ismael), Gunnar Björnstrand (Filip Landahl), Anna Bergman
(Hanna Schwartz), Per Mattson (Mikael Bergman), Nils Brandt
(Morsing), Heinz Hopf (Tomas Graal), Åke Lagergren (Johan
Armfeldt), Lickå Sjöman (Grete Holm), Sune Mangs (Mr.
Salenius), Maud Hyttenberg (Mrs. Sinclair), Kerstin Karte
(prompter), Tore Karte (administrative director), Marianne
Karlbeck (Mrs. Palmgren), Gus Dahlström (set decorator), Gösta
Prüzelius (Dr. Furstenberg), Georg Arlin (colonel), Ernst
Günther (dean of the university), Jan Malmsjö (Bishop Edvard
Vergérus), Kerstin Tidelius (Henrietta Vergérus), Marianne
Aminoff (Mrs. Blenda Vergérus), Marrit Olsson (Malla Tander),
Brita Billsten (Karna), Harriet Andersson (Justina), Krister Hell
(young man 1), Peter Stormare (young man 2), Linda Kruger
(Pauline), Pernilla Wahlgren (Esmeralda), Carl Billquist (police
inspector), Anna Rydberg (Rosa).